Jane Crewdson

Lays of the Reformation

And other lyrics scriptural and miscellaneous

Jane Crewdson

Lays of the Reformation
And other lyrics scriptural and miscellaneous

ISBN/EAN: 9783744797238

Printed in Europe, USA, Canada, Australia, Japan

Cover: Foto ©Thomas Meinert / pixelio.de

More available books at **www.hansebooks.com**

LAYS OF THE REFORMATION

AND OTHER LYRICS,

𝔖criptural and 𝔐iscellaneous.

BY

JANE CREWDSON,

AUTHOR OF

"THE SINGER OF EISENACH," "AUNT JANE'S VERSES FOR CHILDREN," ETC.

LONDON:

HATCHARD AND CO. 187 PICCADILLY.

MDCCCLX.

PREFACE.

NEITHER the compass nor the design of these poems may be found to respond exactly to the promise of the title-page. The " Reformation Lays" do not attempt to present any historical or systematic view of the most important movement in the social history of the world, since the messengers of a new religion first brought the Gospel into Europe. They merely take up, here and there, a stray echo from the voice of history, and give it back in rhyme.

Identified with the Protestant Reformation, there are names which are almost as worthy of our love and gratitude as the honoured name

a

of Luther, yet left unnoticed here. Of these five " Reformation Lays," three concern the great Saxon Reformer, and the fifth, a humble teacher of the Truth, whose proper name was never written on the scroll of history, but whose simple story is verified by more than one contemporaneous authority.*

The first "Lay" requires no comment. The name of Wycliffe, England's own morning star, is dear in almost every British home, wherein a Protestant Bible is held to be the household treasure, and its teachings the household guide.

The second division of this volume consists of subjects exclusively drawn from Holy Scripture. They are not arranged with any view to historical or chronological order.

In dealing with Bible subjects, the writer has constantly been checked by the remembrance of

* See " Histoire Catholique de Notro Temps," par S. Fontaine, Paris, 1562. And also, "Histoire des Eglises Reformées," par Théodore de Beza.

the salutary warning not to aspire to gild pure gold, nor to paint the lily of the field. Such an attempt is sure to result in failure ; and it has therefore been her aim to select, with a reverent hand, such subjects as the pen of inspiration has left in outline, rather than those which have been filled up in detail. Her desire has been not to lower the Bible to familiar thought, but to lift the thought to the Bible.

The third division is composed of very miscellaneous materials. Beginning with some historical pieces, it soon narrows its course into the familiar and the domestic : and here the companionship of the reader is invited in virtue of a common sympathy in weal and woe.

Manchester, December 1859.

CONTENTS.

Lays of the Reformation.

Scripture Lyrics.

Miscellaneous.

LAYS OF THE REFORMATION.

B

" WHEN I recall to mind how the bright and blissful Reformation (by Divine power) struck through the black and settled night of ignorance and antichristian tyranny, methinks a sovereign and reviving joy must needs rush into the bosom of him that reads or hears ; and the sweet odour of the returning Gospel embathe his soul with the fragrancy of heaven. Then was the sacred Bible sought out of the dusty corners where profane falsehood and neglect had thrown it ; the schools opened ; divine and human learning raked out of forgotten tongues ; the princes and critics trooping apace to the new-erected banner of salvation ; the martyrs, with the unresistible might of weakness, shaking the powers of darkness and scorning the fiery rage of the old red dragon."—MILTON.

MORNING STARS.

PART I.

. . . . " He made the stars,
And set them in the firmament of heaven
To illuminate the earth, and rule the day
In their vicissitude, and rule the night,
And light from darkness to divide."

MILTON, *Paradise Lost*, Book 7th.

Now count five hundred rings, or more,

In the bole of the old oak-trees

That wave their broken shadows o'er

The rocky banks of Tees ;

And bid the chronicles of yore

Bring back five centuries.

In Egglestone old Priory [1]

   The lamps are burning dim,

And daylight, with a gentle eye,

   Peeps through the windows trim ;

And the monks are chaunting drowsily

   The sweet old matin hymn.

They chaunt it bravely, note by note,

   Though half asleep they seem;

For they know it every word by rote,

   And could sing it in a dream:

And o'er their pauses softly float

   The voices of the stream.

Betwixt the sculptured traceries

   The tender light is stealing ;

Pouring the quiet of the skies,—

   Like some fresh breath of healing,—

Across the missals' glowing dyes,

   And o'er those figures kneeling.

Down o'er the Abbot's brcidered gown

    It sheds a chastening ray ;

And on the poor monk's shaven crown,

    And coat of hodden grey ;

And o'er the altar trickles down,

    Like blessing dropped astray.

There sits a gentle lady fair,—

    In ancient hall sits she,—

In kirtle edged with miniver,

    And coat of cramoisie :

And a little babe, of beauty rare,

    Is sleeping on her knee.[2]

You might search each Yorkshire dale anear,

    And search afar each wold,

Yet never find that infant's peer,

    So beauteous to behold !

With lambent eye and forehead-clear,

    And hair like thredded gold.

The morning star, so pale and mild,
   Through the old lattice crept,
And shone upon the dreaming child,
   The while he softly slept ;
And the young babe awoke, and smiled,
   As o'er his lip it swept.

The Lady spake out merrily,—
   " Alack, my pretty son !
The star of morn seems claiming thee,[3]
   In earnest, for her own ;
And o'er thy forehead, stealthily,
   Her holy chrism thrown."

Time flew.   The babe at Wycliffe hall[4]
   Like lily, grew apace :
A gentle Boy—the loved of all—
   With sweet, angelic face ;
And a shrewd fancy, held in thrall
   By tender cords of grace.

There sat a grandeur on his brow,

    So pure and undefiled,

Which even made the aged bow

    In reverence to the child.

And now and then there flushed a glow

    Of transport when he smiled.

And day by day this little one

    Hied o'er the craggy hill,

By river side, through forest lone,

    And by the splashing gill ;

That the poor monks at Egglestone

    Might learn him clerkly skill.

Like a pure dewdrop from the sky,

    On scenes of gloom and din ;

Or like a sun-ray from on high,

    This gentle youth dropped in ;

With low, sweet voice, and guileless eye,

    Reproving sloth and sin.

The aged faces grew less old,
　　Scanning his youthful grace ;
The cynic less morose and cold,
　　While gazing on his face ;
Less confident the coarse and bold,
　　And less depraved the base.

That old monk, with the artist eye,
　　And open manuscript,
And glowing palette — patiently
　　Waits — with his pencil dipped,
Until the saintly boy draw nigh
　　The old " Scriptorium" crypt.

With brush 'twixt finger and 'twixt thumb,
　　And gilded vellum spread,
He waits until his model come
　　For the young Baptist's head :
Impatient lest the morning bloom
　　From the boy's cheek be fled.

It was but little they could teach,

Beyond their missal's store ;

But this was written in the speech

The grand old Vulgate bore ;

And Latin words were steps to reach

A higher, holier lore.

" Now, read me not about your saints,

But take this volume down,

Which tells how Christ was railed against,

And wore the thorny crown ;

And how the Lord of glory faints

Upon the cross — alone !

" And read me how the Baptist felt,

When first the Christ he knew ;

And how he gladly would have knelt

To loose his Master's shoe ;

And how he wore the rough hair-belt

O'er loyal heart and true !

" How Jesus raised the ruler's dead,

   And the poor widow's son ;

And how the multitude were fed

   With food, where there was none.

For when God's children cry for bread,

   He doth not give a stone."

The lazy Friars—not a few—

   Swore, by Saint Peter's rood,

That little JOHN DE WYCLIFFE grew

   Too clerkly and too shrewd!

" And some," quoth they, " will live to rue

   This child—so over-good!"

MORNING STARS.

PART II.

" . . . . The morning star of song, who made
His music heard below;
Dan Chaucer, the first warbler, whose sweet breath
Preluded those melodious bursts that fill
The spacious times of great Elizabeth
With sounds that echo still."— TENNYSON.

Two moving shadows slowly glide

Forth from the sylvan shade!

Two youths are pacing, side by side,

Up Thorsgill's broomy glade!

The woodland creatures scarcely hide —

The shy are scarce afraid.

Two pleasant voices, young and free,
    In earnest converse blend ;
Yet neither seemeth to agree,
    In counsel, with his friend ;
And though they commune courteously,
    They neither yield nor bend.

The accent of the younger shames
    The northman's simple tongue ;
It smatters of the banks of Thames,
    And of the joust and song ;
And of the courtly London dames,
    The dance, and festive throng.

He wears a camlet rochet grand,
    Broider'd with golden thread —
A jewell'd ring on dainty hand,
    And pointed hosen red ;
And a jaunty cap, with plume and band,
    Placed sidewise on his head ; —

A merry youth!—And yet, o'er all,

 The soul immortal glanced;

And genius spurned at fashion's thrall,

 And loved the Muses' haunts.

And on those lips, refined and small,

And eyes like Amadis' of Gaul,

 The soul of song lay tranced.

He had quaff'd largely at the well

 Of sweet Provençal lore;

And just had found a hollow shell

 Upon his native shore :—

And almost started at the swell

 Of song which floated o'er!

Quoth he, " Dear WYCLIFFE! those are wise,

 And I a frolic youth;

Yet both hate falsehood and disguise,

 And both revere the truth:[5]

Thou, a true saint, with those pure eyes,

 And I—no saint, forsooth!

" Oh, I would sweep my country's lyre,

 With daring hand and free,

And tune to song each stubborn wire,

 Till men shall say of me,

' DAN CHAUCER is the princely sire

 Of England's poesy !'

" Ah, I will such, like honey-bee,

 The flowers of fair Provence ;

And steal, from Guillaume de Lorris,

 The Rose's quaint romance ;[6]

And sip my pipe of Malvoisie

 In Windsor's royal haunts.

" I'll pledge thy health in jewell'd cup,

 Thou saintly Gospeler !

When Percy and when Chaucer sup

 With noble Lancaster.[7]

Ah, those old monks !—we'll show them up,

 And lash each lazy *frère*."

He laughed a jocund peal ; — it rung
    Adown the forest glen ;
The woodpecker, with flippant tongue,
    Laughed merrily again ;
The heron from the river sprung,
    The bittern from the fen.

" Alas, Sir Bard ! Thy stinging dart
    May scar the Dragon's skin ;
But will not reach the evil heart,
    Nor mend the life within.
He'll writhe a moment at the smart,
    But only hug the sin.

" 'Tis not thy laugh — 'tis not my sigh —
    Nor frolic jest — nor frown —
Can Antichrist, in strength, defy,
    And smite his banner down:
The Saviour must be lifted high,
    Ere Sin be overthrown.

" God give me grace !— I will not grant
    Sloth to my labouring breast
Until His Ark of Covenant
    Shall find a place of rest ;
And England's hills and dales shall pant
    For blessings — *and be bless'd.*

" I'll open wide a living brook
    On every barren moor ;
I'll take the Gospel's holy book,
    And give it to the poor ;
And blind men on the light shall look,
    And, seeing Christ, adore !

" From where the Loire in sunshine flows
    Thou bring'st the quaint ' *Romaunt;* '
And of the worldling's vapid woes,
    Dear Bard ! thou lov'st to chaunt:
But *I* would pluck sweet Sharon's Rose,
And wheresoe'er the poor man goes
    That fragrant flower I'd plant.

" I'd pour soft drops of Gilead's balm

    O'er every wounded head ;

I'd wave the victor's holy palm

    O'er every dying bed ;

And laud, and prayer, and dulcet psalm,

The troubled soul shall cheer and calm,

    In native language read."

" Forsooth !—Thy saintship's reveries

    My poet-dreams outshine !

But, ah ! I'd creep on bended knees

    To old Saint Becket's shrine ;

And I would scatter to the breeze

The choicest pearls of Indian seas—

Aye, give my sweetest melodies—

    For one such dream as thine !"

They part.—Life's river soon shall fret

    And brawl betwixt the twain,.

c

And many a sun of hope shall set,

And many a star shall wane ;

And laurel wreaths with tears be wet,

Ere clasp they hands again !

MORNING STARS.

PART III.

" Our Wycliffe's preaching was the lamp at which all the
succeeding reformers lighted their tapers."— MILTON.

A SINGLE horseman, from a lane,

    Is ambling into sight !—

With jewell'd hand he checks the rein

    Of palfrey, sleek and white,

To listen to the merle's refrain,

Until those troubled eyes again -

    O'erflow with frolic light.

The palfrey crops the linden spray,
　　Dripping with dews of eve.
The rider's fingers softly play
　　With threads of thought — to weave
A dewy stanza, in a lay,
　　About a " Flower and Leaf!"[8]

Time hath pass'd roughly, with his plough,
　　Across that face of care,
And grooved deep furrows on the brow,
　　Still grand with genius rare ;
As if the envied laurel bough
　　Distill'd but poison there !

Anon, the curfew's mellow chime
　　Floats from an old church-tower —
The poet drops his threaded rhyme
　　About the Leaf and Flower ;
And, chafing at the waste of time,
　　Leaves fancy's dewy bower.

The sweet " Amen" seem'd lingering still
    Around the house of prayer—
The breath of praise seem'd yet to fill
    The balmy, sunset air—
As, o'er the brook and up the hill,
    The scatter'd people fare.

The poet wondered to behold
    The light of gentle grace,
Which shone, as from a lamp of gold,
    On every peasant's face :
A look of holy peace, that told
The flock had found the shepherd's fold,
    A quiet resting-place !

The halt and aged seemed to lean
    Upon some secret stay ;
The heavy-laden to have seen
    Their burden rolled away ;
The solaced mourner to have been
    Where she could weep and pray.

Like picture of some saint of yore,

In Gothic niche portrayed,

The preacher, from the low-arched door,

Emerges from the shade :

While sunset glories, floating o'er,

A golden nimbus, softly pour

Around his snow-white head.

Like pilgrims met at eventide

To pitch the desert tent ;

Like aged brothers, parted wide,

To meet when day is spent ;

The friends are seated, side by side,

In converse eloquent.9

" WYCLIFFE ! How soft the shadows lay

Beneath those summer trees,

When we twain dreamed our dreams one day,

Beside the banks of Tees !

E'en as that stream, in reckless play,

Tossed to the winds its foamy spray,

So have I tossed life's wine away,

    And sucked the bitter lees.

" Though kings have twined my laureate wreath,

    And warriors sung my praise ;

Though time hath breathed immortal breath

    Upon my deathless lays ;

And princes crouched to bask beneath

    The sparkle of my rays ;

" 'Twas only while my merry jest

    Could brim the festal bowl,

And while my witty laugh gave zest

    To the dull worldling's *rôle,*

That CHAUCER's jewelled baldrick pressed

    Across this troubled soul.

" 'Twas all a dream !   Life's only truth
    Was once,—in stormy fight,
When stood the friend of Geoffrey's youth,
    Braving the crozier's might ;
And the court-poet, bland and smooth,
Defied man's threat, and scorned his ruth,
    And stood by WYCLIFFE's right.[10]

" The dream was o'er !   I woke at last
    To find the laurel crown
Shiv'ring in autumn's stormy blast,
    Blighted, and sere, and brown ;
And from my lute—mine idol—passed
    The glory and renown.

" Like a tired child, come home at night,
    With lagging, faltering tread ;
(His hollow reed in tuneless plight,
    His flowers all dank and dead,)
I come to borrow of thy light,
    To find my way to bed !"

Ah! who shall tell what holy cheer
    Came down, like summer rain?
How heavenly love cast out earth's fear,
    With all its shadowy train?
And how the Lord of grace drew near,
    And talkèd with the twain?

Like travellers who appoint a tryst,
    Before they part in love,
Minded to meet again in Christ,
    Within the courts above,
The Poet and Evangelist
    On severed pathways move.

Time passed. The gales of midnight sigh
    Among the churchyard trees:
The wailing streamlet murmurs by,
    Tost by the gusty breeze;
And Seraph-hosts are drawing nigh,
To hail, with "Alleluias" high,
    The fettered saint's release.

Ah ! if men's eyes were finely skilled
    To scan immortal things,
They'd see his dying chamber filled
    With angels' radiant wings ;
And if their plaintive sighs were stilled,
Perchance the ear of faith were thrilled
    With sounds from viewless strings.

Time passed.   The trysting-place drew near,
    The holy tryst was kept :
And princes thronged around the bier
    Where England's Poet slept ;
And strangers came to drop a tear,
    And merrie England wept.

They scooped their minstrel's narrow grave
    Among the royal dead ;
And the banners of the mighty wave
    Around his laureled head ;
And the scutcheons of the proud and brave
    Glow round his dreamless bed.

The Poet left to earth,—" a well
  Of English undefiled :"[11]
A place to gather asphodel
  For every minstrel child !
Alas ! that e'er its babblings tell,
Of baneful flower and noxious bell,
  And gropings through a wild.

Each left his legacy.   The saint
  Left glorious wealth untold,
More than the mind of man can paint,
  And more than eyes behold :
To poor—and lone—and sick—and faint,
  Pearls—silver—finest gold !

He opened wide a living brook
  By cot and cabin door ;
He made the Gospel's holy Book
  Speak peace from shore to shore ;
The bread of life from Christ he took,
  And gave it to the poor.

He lit Truth's lamp, at dead of night,

   With patient toil and skill ;

He bore it bravely through the fight,

   And set it on a hill.

And distant watchers hailed the sight,

And lit their torch at WYCLIFFE's light,

   —And, lo ! it burneth still ! [12]

NOTES.

NOTE 1, page 4.

" In Egglestone old Priory."

The ruins of Egglestone Priory, or Abbey (for Tanner calls it the latter and Leland the former), are beautifully situated upon the angle formed by a little dell called Thorsgill, at its junction with the river Tees. The Priory is supposed to have been founded about the end of the reign of Henry the Second.

NOTE 2, page 5.

" And a little babe, of beauty rare,
    Is sleeping on her knee."

Most of the portraits professing to be likenesses of Wycliffe indicate a high style of beauty, both in feature and in expression. Probably not one is an original likeness: but in the portraits of celebrated men there has generally been some remote, historical picture, or description, from which copyists have originally worked.

Note 3, page 6.

" The star of morn seems claiming thee."

About the same transition-period from darkness to daylight, arose England's two Morning Stars.   In 1324 was
born John Wycliffe, in an obscure Yorkshire valley on the
banks of the Tees.   In 1326 .was born Geoffrey Chaucer,
on the banks of the Thames.   Both were " *Morning Stars.*"
The one ushered in the dawn of religious reformation and
liberty of conscience, the other was the father of English
poetry.   To compare the heavenly vocation of the former
with the intellectual services of the latter would seem folly,
excepting in so far as they both contended (though with
very different weapons) for truth, and both for the un-
masking of falsehood.   Moreover, they both contributed to
settle and fix the noble language of their native land, then
capriciously fluctuating between the Norman-French and
the Anglicised Saxon.   Wycliffe, by his translation of the
Bible into fine old Saxon-English, gave to the common
people the Word of Truth in the language of hearth and
home.   Chaucer, by his courtly diction, drawn from the
polished South as well as from the sterner North, imparted
just that richness and flexibility which were needed to
commend his native tongue to the peer as well as to the
peasant, and to prove its adaptation for general literature.

Note 4, page 6.

" Time flew.   The babe at Wycliffe hall."

Dr. Whittaker, in his *History of Richmondshire*, pain-
fully disputes the general impression respecting the place

of Wycliffe's birth. His arguments, however, scarcely un-
settle the current opinion; namely, that the great Forerunner
of the Protestant Reformation was born at *Wycliffe Hall*, on
the banks of the Tees, near Barnard Castle.

Note 5, page 13.

" Yet both hate falsehood and disguise,
       And both revere the truth."

That the Poet sympathised with the Gospel Doctor in
many of his enlightened religious opinions is an historical
fact.

Note 6, page 14.

" And steal, from Guillaume de Lorris,
       The Rose's quaint romance."

The celebrated old poem called *The Romaunt of the
Rose* was translated by Chaucer into English metre, from
the old French of Guillaume de Lorris.

Note 7, page 14.

" I'll pledge thy health in jewell'd cup,
       Thou saintly Gospeler!
When Percy and when Chaucer sup
       With noble Lancaster."

John of Gaunt, the princely Duke of Lancaster, was the
patron of the Poet as well as the protector of the Reformer ;
and Chaucer heartily entered into the Duke's espousal of
Wycliffe's cause.

NOTE 8, page 20.

" A dewy stanza, in a lay,
About a ' *Flower and Leaf*.' "

See Chaucer's Poems. The fable of " the Flower and
the Leaf" is an exquisite thing—fresh and dewy.

NOTE 9, page 22.

" The friends are seated, side by side,
In converse eloquent."

That there really existed a personal friendship betwixt
the twain (in other words, that the " Morning Stars" sometimes loved to sing together) may be further guessed by
Chaucer's lovely description of a true Gospel Minister of
his times, said to be a portrait, from the life, of the Rector
of Lutterworth. The features are limned in with such a
loving hand, that it seems impossible to doubt their truth-
fulness.

" A good man of religion did I see,
And a poor parson of a town was he:
But rich he was of holy thought and work,
And also was a learned man—a clerk,
And truly would Christ's holy gospel preach,
And his parishioners devoutly teach.
Benign he was, and wondrous diligent,
And patient when adversity was sent.

*   *   *   *   *

Wide was his parish—houses far asunder—
But he neglected nought for rain or thunder.

In sickness and in grief to visit all,
The farthest in his parish, great and small ·
Always on foot, and in his hand a stave.

    *   *   *   *   *

And though he holy was, and virtuous,
He was to sinful men full piteous.
His words were strong, but not with anger fraught;
A love benignant he distinctly taught.
To draw mankind to heaven by gentleness
And good example, was his business.
But if that any one were obstinate,
Whether he were of high or low estate ;
Him would he sharply check with altered mien ;
A better parson there was no where seen.
He paid no court to pomps or reverence,
Nor spiced his conscience at his soul's expence ;
But Jesu's love, which owns no pride or pelf,
He taught,—*but first he followed it himself.*"

Note 10, page 24.

" 'Twas all a dream !   Life's only truth
   Was once,—in stormy fight,
When stood the friend of Geoffrey's youth,
   Braving the crozier's might ;
And the court-poet, bland and smooth,
Defied man's threat, and scorned his ruth,
   And stood by WYCLIFFE's right."

There is an interesting historical picture by Egan, en-
graved by Jones, in which is represented the citation of
Wycliffe (in Saint Paul's) to answer the charge of heresy.

Geoffrey Chaucer's poet-face may be seen in close proximity
to the beautiful countenance of the Rector of Lutterworth.

Note 11, page 27.

" The Poet left to earth,—' a well
Of English undefiled.' "

" Dan Chaucer! well of English undefiled."— SPENSER.

Note 12, page 28.

" He lit Truth's lamp, at dead of night,
With patient toil and skill;
He bore it bravely through the fight,
And set it on a hill.
And distant watchers hailed the sight,
And lit their torch at WYCLIFFE's light,
—And, lo! it burneth still!"

Milton, in one of his prose essays, truly remarks, " Our
Wycliffe's preaching was the lamp at which all the succeeding reformers lighted their tapers."

The lamp never went out. It shone across the sea to
the continent of Europe; and was welcomed with a response
from Alpine fastnesses and Bohemian forests. 'Till, at
length, the great Saxon Reformer awoke, and, with his
powerful voice, proclaimed the daylight.

THE SCHLOSS-KIRCHE DOOR.

(AN OLD MONK'S TALE.)

Luther affixed his celebrated Theses to the door of the
old Schloss-Kirche at Wittenberg, on the eve of All Saints'
Day, 1517.

" THE Seller of Indulgences,

    With all his pampered band,

Had trafficked with his deadly ware

    Throughout the Saxon's land ;—

The Saxon's land, where towers are strong,

    And wills and deeds are bold ;

And honest hearts shall never be

Turned by the wards of any key,

    Of iron or of gold !

" The Seller of Indulgences
    Was worthy of his craft ;
He took away the people's gold,
    And left the poison-draught.
He took away the people's wealth
    To gild Saint Peter's dome,
But left a shaft with force unspent,
Whose pointed barb should back be sent —
    By a strong arm — to Rome !

" 'Twas not the soft and jewelled hand
    Of Kaiser or of King,
Which laid the arrow on the bow,
    And pulled the whirring string.
'Twas not a hand in glove of steel
    Made strong by sturdy fight ;
Nor yet the pale and sinewy hand
That wields the gilded crozier-wand,
    With proud, yet borrowed might.

" It was an arm well nerved for fight,
  And strong to will and dare —
A poor monk's feeble hand, made strong
  By lifting up in prayer !
By drawing down its secret might
  From treasuries unfailing ;
Wrestling, like Jacob, all night long,
Halting and weak, while waxing strong,
  And, as a prince, prevailing !*

" He rose up from his knees one eve —
  (Methinks I see him now,
With autumn's stormy twilight poured
  Upon his massive brow)—
Dashed down his book of popish prayers,
  Recoiling with a start :
And, with a loving grasp, then took
Another and a holier Book,
  And girt it on his heart.

* Genesis, xxxii. 28.

" I marked a sparkle of the eye,
    A freedom in each move,
Like what I've seen in champion knight
    When he throws down his glove.
The miner's son might match the knight,
    In gesture and in tone :
I know not how, but so it was,
The poor Augustine monk might pass
    For a highborn baron's son.

" Ah me !   No knight with plume and lance,
    E'er played a sterner *rôle!*
His morion was the convent cowl,
    His glove a written scroll —
A scroll whose every line was writ
    Mid sighs, and tears, and prayer :
And midnight's shade, and twilight's gleam,
And noontide's clear, unwavering beam,
    All left their pathway there.

" Along the convent corridor

   He strode, with steady pace —

The Brothers peeping from their cells

   To gaze upon his face.

And some did frown a scowl that well

   Might all heaven's saints dishearten :

But others raised their drooping head,

And wrung his hand, and whispering said,

   ' Christ bless thee, *Brother Martin!*'

" And then adown the old oak stairs,

   With muffled sandal shod,

He passed — and every ancient board

   Creaked harshly as he trod.

And out into the cloistered court,

   And 'neath the portal low ;

And there the shades seemed backward driven,

And the pure, liquid light of heaven

   Streamed right upon his brow.

" Alone he trod the gabled street,
    For men took little heed,
As yet, of what was Gospel truth,
    And what the Romish creed.
Ithuriel had not touched the foe,
    As yet, with fiery spear ;
And made him shift his old disguise,
And starting from his lair, arise
    In sin's true character.

" October's stormy evening sky
    Lit up the old Schloss-Kirk,
And threw a crimson gleam adown
    The stony tracery-work ;
Pouring a broken ray aslant
    Across the dusky aisle :
And, in the western portal dim,
Making the demon-masks look grim,
    And stony saints to smile.

" He stood beneath the heavy arch,
    In the full ruddy light ;
And with his left hand grasped a nail,—
    A hammer with his right :—
Unrolled that scroll he writ with tears,
    And signed midst heaving groans :—
Rapp, rapp !—oh, door of Saxon oak !
Didst ever quail with such a stroke,
E'er since the woodman's hatchet woke
    The echoes with thy moans ?

" I shuddered as the vaulted aisle
    Gave back the hollow sound ;
And every shrine obeyed the sign,
    And sent the echo round.
Rapp, rapp !—a second nail is driven,
    Too firm for storms to move !
Rapp, rapp !—a third !—a fourth !—all right !
Hurrah for Europe's champion-knight !
    He hath thrown down the glove !

" When convent-chapel lamps were lit
      That eve, for vesper prayer,
No sweet voice chaunted forth the psalm
      So strong as his, so rare!
'Twould seem as if the burdened soul
      Had brought her weary load
Of hopes and fears, of gain and loss,
And Faith had nailed *all* to the cross,
      And left it there with God.

" The winter sun uprose next morn,
      Cold, cloudless, and serene ;
Smiling a silvery smile of peace
      Across the frosty scene.
The old Schloss-Kirk, in festal pomp,
      Soon oped her portals wide ;
And lines of priests, in grand array,
Spread out the relics for display,
To edify, on ' All Saints' Day,'
      The neighbouring country side.

" From many a hamlet's quiet shade,

   From many a storm-rent tower,

From forest path, and river's brink,

   And peaceful vintage bower ;

On slow-paced mule, on prancing steed,

   On holy pilgrim staff,

They throng the gates, within, without,

And make the old walls ring with shout,

   And song, and psalm, and laugh.

" But song, and psalm, and laughter-shout

   Are changed for grave debate,

Soon as that giddy multitude

   Have reached the old Kirk-gate,

And spy those *Theses*, lettered out

   Clear, legible, and strong.

The clerkly con them o'er and o'er,

The learnèd read them to the poor,

And, halting round the grey Kirk-door,

   Cluster the gathering throng.

" The baron smiled a puzzled smile ;
    His lady laughed outright—
For woman's heart is always quick
    To catch a ray of light.
The friars shook their shaven crowns —
    ' The monk is mad,' quoth one —
But others sighed, ' If *he* be mad,
Augustine the like mania had,
    And Paul, and sweet Saint John !'

" A pilgrim smote upon his breast,—
    ' I might have prayed at home,
Nor dragged my weary, heavy heart,
    And bleeding feet, to Rome !'
' Alack !' responds a burgher's dame,
    Betwixt a smile and scowl,—
' I might have kept (and been no worse)
Those golden guelders in my purse,
Nor heaped, perchance, another curse
    Upon poor Tetzel's soul.'

" But, ah ! the smile of radiant joy
　　Which lit the poor man's eye !
' Is there indulgence, then, for *me*
　　Who have no gold to buy ?
They told me that my lost one lies
　　In purgatorial flame,
Because I had no coin, alas !
To buy a single priestly mass,
　　To save my one ewe lamb.'

" In vain the swinging censer's breath
　　Perfumes the heavy air ;
And round the altar's glittering height
　　A hundred tapers glare.
In vain the choral anthem swells,
　　Their truant hearts to win ;
And pompous sacristans in vain
Sweep the long aisle with rustling train,
　　To lure the people in.

" Still, still around the old Kirk-door,
    In loud debate they stand—
The posies for the Virgin's shrine
    Slow withering in their hand.
That morn one strong electric shock
    Hath touched a thousand strings—
That morn the deathless soul awoke,
And started from beneath man's yoke
    To find that she hath wings !

" Ah me !   Full many a year hath flown,
    And many a tempest's stroke
Hath struck, and back recoiled again
    From that old door of oak :
Yet, though an old man's eyes wax dim,
    And memory halts and fails,
And ears grow dull, methinks I hear,
In strong distinctness, bold and clear,
    That hammer on those nails.

" O'er vale and hill, o'er mount and plain,
  The booming echoes roll,
Knocking against the dungeon doors
  Of man's imprisoned soul.
The dark pine-forests caught the sound,
  The hills replied again ;
The mountains sped it on its flight,
And tossed it on from height to height,
  And rolled it to the plain.

" Old Tyber frets his tawny wave,
  And chafes with muddy foam,
To speed the Vandal note of war
  On to the gates of Rome.
The seven hills awake from sleep,
  Affrighted at the peal ;
And turning fiercely at the sound,
Old Antichrist receives a wound
  Which never more shall heal.

" Long since, I left my convent cell,
　　For Christ, who made me free ;
To preach His gospel to the poor,
　　In glorious liberty ;
To pray the spirit-prayer of faith
　　Without the senseless beads ;
To grasp the living Word of Light,
In all its quickening truth and might,
　　Without man's deadening creeds.

" Ah ! I can think on Him who bled
　　Upon th' accursed tree,
Without the graven crucifix
　　To help my memory.
Without the mass-book I can laud
　　His grace, on bended knees ;
And when my spirit plumes her wing,
Without my missal I can sing
　　Sweet ' *Benedicites !* ' "

LUTHER AT WORMS,

IN 1521.

" Ein feste Burg ist unser Gott,
   Ein gute Wehr und Waffen,
Er helft uns frei aus aller Noth
   Die uns je hat betroffen."
                                LUTHER.

THUS spake a youthful warrior,
   In the knightly days of old,—
With mirthful eye, and open brow,
   And step erect and bold :—
" Sit here, and tell me, grandsire,
   Some tale of daring deed ;
Of hero, girt with charmèd sword,
   Bridling his fiery steed !

Tell of the scaly dragon,[1]

   'Neath Siegfred's mighty hand —

The glory and the darling of

   The German's Fatherland !

How with a thousand plaudits,

   The dark pine-forests rang,

And ancient minstrels wove the lays

   Which fair young maidens sang."

The old man paused — high visions

   Upon his soul throng fast ;

And memory's touch is wandering o'er

   The key-notes of the Past.

And when he spake, sonorous

   Became his voice, and clear —

Unlike the weak and faltering tones

   The youth was wont to hear.

" I'll tell thee of a hero,

   Before whose pure renown,

Down to the dust falls each sere leaf

    From Siegfred's lordly crown!

I'll tell thee of a braver

    Than all whose knightly praise

Is registered in chronicle,

    Or chaunted forth in lays.

Aye, boy! the *free soul's* champion!

    Who wielded such a brand,

As dauntless Siegfred never grasped

    Within his steel-gloved hand;

And dealt the old Arch-dragon

    A blow—so sturdily!—

That a thousand, thousand captive souls

    Were from his coil set free.

" It was a spring-tide morning?—

    I mind me how the vine

Was putting forth her tender leaves,

    Along the winding Rhine;

And how the silvery blossoms
 Were budding on the thorn ;
And sprouted on the upland slopes,
 The young blades of the corn.

" But the peasant left his vineyard,
 And the lady left her bower,
And the baron, on his stout roan steed,
 Spurred down from castled tower ;
And the smith forsook his anvil,
 And boys forgot their play,
To throng this old imperial town
 Upon that wondrous day.

" Ah me !   I was a stripling ;
 And my father's vassals said
That chestnut ringlets never waved
 Upon a comelier head ;
And that the broidered doublet
 Ne'er spanned a nobler chest ;

And that a fleeter step ne'er chased
    The leveret from her nest.

" I went forth on that morning
    A child of careless glee,
To whom the whole world seemed a dream
    Of song and revelry !
There came a change ere sunset:
    And the mirthful, heedless youth
Awoke, henceforth to look on life
As a holy battle-field of strife,
    Of earnestness and truth !

" I had seen the youthful Kaiser,[3]
    And gave admiring heed
To the housings, wrought in blue and gold,
    Of his Andalusian steed :
I had marked his lordly bearing,
    And owned the stern appeal

Of the Austrian lip, astute and firm,
    And proud eye of Castile.
I had seen his Flemish warriors,
    With plume and gilded spur ;
And pampered Andalusian lords,
    In silk and miniver.
My eyes were dazed with gazing
    On corslet and on helm,
As they thronged the city's northern gate,
And passed in slow, imperial state,
    To the Diet of the realm.
But it was not prince nor pageant
    That wrought my spirit's change,
And Kaiser Karl was not the man
    To move a work so strange.

" The Herald of the empire,*
    Robed in official garb,

Had sped on high commission forth,

    Upon his milk-white barb.

He forded many a river,

    Crossed many a mountain-chain,

And threaded many a forest-path,

    And scoured o'er many a plain.

He passed by princely castles,

    And cities of renown,

But paused — before the lowly gate

    Of a grey old Saxon town!

The rude and rugged pavement

    Is ringing 'neath his feet,

As the milk-white barb is pacing slow

    Along the dusky street.

All knew that rider's mission,

    And why he came in state,

And drew his rein, and bent his plume

    Beneath the convent-gate: —

For a strong voice, from that portal,

    Had echoed far and near,

And had mutter'd 'mongst the seven hills,
 And made Rome quake for fear!—
Aye!—from a poor monk's cloister
 A tempest had been hurl'd,
Whose mighty heavings were to shake
 The prison of a world!

 " ' Thy Kaiser, *Martin Luther!*
 And the Diet of the State,
Do cite thee thither to repair
 Within a certain date.
He covenants ' Safe-Conduct,'
 And, to assure thy weal,
He signs the mandate with his name,
 And seals it with his seal.'

 " There was sighing in the cloister,
 There was wailing in the town:—
' Alas! our Brother goeth forth
 To win the martyr's crown!

We've heard of perjur'd councils —
    Of violated bond —
And of the plighted, broken troth
    Of Kaiser Sigismond ! ' [5]

" But, 'midst the reeds that trembled
    Before the gathering storm,
E'en like some deeply-rooted oak
    Stood Luther's dauntless form.   .
Exultant amidst peril,
    Forth goes he to fulfil —
In face of friend, in face of foe —
    God's and his Kaiser's will.[6]

" Oh the throbbings of men's bosoms,
    Oppress'd by doubt and fear ! —
Oh the surgings of the multitude,
    As that poor monk drew near !

From hamlet and from city
   Around his feet they press;—
Some came to curse the heretic,
   And some the saint to bless.
' Cursed be the bold arch-rebel!'
   Was mutter'd 'mongst the crowd;
' God bless the man whom Rome hath cursed!'
   Responded clear and loud.
And many a peasant-mother—
   At cot, or cabin-door—
Held up her little babe, to see
   The teacher of the Poor.

" I mind me how I mingled
   Amongst the eddying throng,
And how my youthful steps were borne
   With torrent force along.—
I mind me how the Herald
   Pranced, foremost in the band,

And the Empire's Eagle spread its wings
 Upon his gilded wand ; —
And next, my young eye singled,
 From out the troublous scene,
One steadfast brow, *one* fearless eye,
 One calm, heroic mien —
A rock, whose base the surges
 Swept round, but could not move —
Conversing with his soul within,
 And with his God above !

" With that one look, fast faded
 Life's pageantry away ! —
Aye, Boy ! the masquerade was o'er —
 I gazed no more that day !

" Uprose the dewy morning,

    And gemm'd the vines with pearl,

And waken'd to their matin-song

    The throstle and the merle —

Waken'd the troublous city

    To the battle-field of life,

And woke the monk of Wittenberg

    To the trumpet-call of strife.

Uprose the weary princes

    From brief, perturb'd repose :

And from his purple couch of state

    Young Kaiser Charles arose !

" Bring forth the golden flagons,

    And pour the red wine free ;

And fill your goblets to the brim,

    From casks of Burgundy !

And for the lists now nerve ye,

    At yon imperial board,

And in the lordly banquet-hall
   Be your dull strength restored!
For Rome's unconquer'd rebel
   Hath weapons well anneal'd;
And his girdle he is bracing *now*,
   And polishing his shield!

" He hath enterèd his closet,
   And, kneeling prostrate there,
He is pouring forth his troubled soul
   In sighs, and tears, and prayer![7]
God help thee, Martin Luther!
   Thy Lord hath hid His face,
And, for a season, sealèd up
   The treasury of grace.
Oh, how the strong man wrestled!—
   Oh, how the weak man cried!—
But he knows the Angel's " Secret Name,"
   And will not be denied.[8]

Amidst thick clouds of darkness,

He knows that name is LOVE,

And that the anchorage of faith

Nor earth nor hell can move!

" I mind me how I marvelled,

As I stood without, and heard

The pleadings of that broken heart,

And how my soul was stirr'd.

I knew not, then, the dealings

Of a Father with a Son ;

Nor how, apart from carnal strength,

The victory is won.

If sever'd from the mighty,

How weak the strong !—how faint !—

And, parted from the Saviour,

How helpless is the Saint !

" But the footstep of the herald

   Is ringing on the stair!—

The hour hath struck, and at its call

   He rises up from prayer.9

Like ocean, whose wild tumult

   Is hush'd at summer even,

Now calmly on his settled brow

   Resteth the light of heaven.

Behold, once more, the Dauntless

   With firm step moves along!—

He feels the *Rock* beneath his feet,

   And therefore is he strong.

" I ween that earth ne'er witnessed

   So lordly an array

Of princes and of potentates

   As met in state that day—

From the banks of yellow Tyber,

   From Danube's moaning river,

From Weser, Elbe, and Vistula,
  And flowery Guadalquiver : [10]
There were stout Teutonic barons,
  And proud Castilian lords,
And Belgic and Burgundian knights,
  Clanking their jewell'd swords ;
There was cloth of gold from Flanders,
  Pearls from the Indian main,
And silks from Asiatic looms,
  And a new world's gold from Spain.

" The Empire's seven Electors, [11]
  Each in his chair of state,
Next to their Kaiser's gilded throne,
  In proud precedence, sate.
I mark'd our youthful monarch,
  Beneath his purple dome,
As whisper'd in his listening ear
  The Legate priest from Rome.

I marked the cruel cunning

    That lit Duke Alva's eye,

And the cloud across the anxious brow

    Of noble Saxony.[12]

" ' Will he retract ?'—Behold him,

    Before ye dare respond !—

Is *that* a man to league with Truth,

    And then to break his bond ?—

To turn again to darkness—

    Back, from the light of day—

To find a pearl of priceless worth,

    And fling that pearl away ?

" ' Wilt thou renounce thy doctrines ?'

    ' Yea !—should they not accord

With Truth unchangeable, declared

    In God's unerring Word.

The mind of man is erring,

   Though honest be its aim —

The mind of God infallibly,

   Immutably, *the same!*

Prove ye that Christ and Luther

   Two gospels do declare,

And Luther's voice shall be the first

   His tenets to forswear ;

But, failing this, my conscience

   Will not, and dare not, yield

To any Standard but the Lord's,

   In any battle-field !

Try, by God's word, each doctrine

   I've taught by speech or pen. —

My Kaiser ! — *here I take my stand,*

   God helping me ! — *Amen !*' [13]

" There was silence in the council,

   And men with awe look'd pale,

And cruel Alva knit his brow,

    And the Legate priest did quail.

'Twas strange!—*Here* sate a monarch,

    'Neath whose imperial sway

(Own'd in two earthly hemispheres)

    Ne'er sets the light of day ;

And *here*, earth's rich and noble—

    Helms, mitres, coronets—

Back'd by the golden bribes of Rome,

    And. failing these, her threats !

And *there*, before his judges,

    Upheld by voice of none,

Stood a poor monk from Wittenberg—

    A simple miner's son—

Leaning upon an anchor,

    Within the riven veil,

And clasping to his breast the Word

    That cannot change nor fail !

" Thus, like some Alpine summit,
        Calm in the light of heaven,
While, round its agitated base,
        Dark thunder-clouds are driven :
In peace, though 'sieged by tempests —
        'Midst tumult, yet at rest —
There stood the man whom Rome hath curst,
        But whom his Lord hath blest !

" Will he retract ? — First turn ye
        The planets from their course,
Or dash the mighty cataract
        Back to its mountain-source !

" My tale is well-nigh ended —
        The Empire's heavy ban

Hath echoed back the thundering curse
   Hurl'd from the Vatican !
What boots man's wrath ? — The banner
   Of Christ hath been unfurl'd,
And a poor Saxon monk becomes
   The Hero of a world !

" The Branded and the Outcast
   A refuge-tower hath found,
Where — Patmos-like — the pen is free,
   And the wing'd soul unbound :
And where the holy Volume,
   Seal'd up, from age to age,
(For only priests and letter'd men
   Could read its learned page)
Became the poor man's treasure,
   Unroll'd by Luther's hand,
And vocal with the living speech
   Of the German's Fatherland —

The speech in which the mother
  Doth with her child converse—
The speech in which the silver-hair'd
  Life's toils and cares rehearse.

" And thus Truth's lamp was lifted,
  By God's o'erruling will,
From shadows of a convent-cell
  And set upon a hill.
It hath lighten'd northern forests,
  It hath smiled in Alpine glens,
And the valleys of the Island Queen
  Have shouted glad ' Amens !'

" The curse, the ban, the Wartburg,
  But veil'd God's glorious ways ;
And the echo to the wrath of man
  Is heard in songs of praise ! [14]

" Aye, Boy !— the mightiest weapon

   Is not thy steel-wrought sword :

The bravest warrior of his age

   Is the servant of the Lord!"

NOTES.

Note 1, page 50.

" Tell of the scaly dragon,
    'Neath Siegfred's mighty hand."

According to the *Niebelungenlied*, it was on the borders of the Rhine, nearly opposite the present city of Worms, that Siegfred, the favourite hero of song and story, destroyed the dragon.

Note 2, page 51.

" It was a spring-tide morning."

It was in spring, on the morning of the 16th of April, 1521, that Luther arrived at Worms, where the Diet had already been sitting more than three months.

Note 3, page 53.

" I had seen the youthful Kaiser."

The Emperor Charles V. was born at Ghent in 1500, and

was, therefore, twenty-one years of age at the period of this celebrated Diet. He was the eldest son of Philip, archduke of Austria, and of Joanna, the daughter of Ferdinand of Arragon and Isabella of Castile.

Note 4, page 54.

" The Herald of the empire."

Everlasting blessings to the soul of the imperial herald, Gaspar Sturm, were the consequences of this mission. His intercourse with Luther during the journey, and Luther's sermons at Weimar, at Eisenach, and at Erfurth, in all which places he was permitted to preach, wrought so powerfully on his convictions, that from henceforth Gaspar Sturm was a staunch friend of Luther and of the Reformation. When Luther left Worms to return to Saxony, the herald joined him again at Oppenheim, near Frankfurt, and accompanied him as far as Freundsberg. There they parted as dear brothers in Christ.

Note 5, page 57.

" We've heard of perjur'd councils —
Of violated bond —
And of the plighted, broken troth
Of Kaiser Sigismond !"

John Huss, the great Bohemian reformer, was executed at Constance, July 7th, 1415, notwithstanding a formal " safe-conduct" from the Emperor Sigismond.

Note 6, page 57.

"Exultant amidst peril,
　Forth goes he to fulfil —
In face of friend, in face of foe —
　God's and his Kaiser's will."

Luther's ready and determined obedience to the imperial summons, in the face alike of warning and of threat, unfolds a noble example of Christian intrepidity. Even the most stout-hearted of his friends implored him to take warning from the history of the past, and abide in a place of safety. But Luther knew that the hour was come for setting the candle upon the candlestick, that it might give light to the world; and his own life was only dear to him as an offering to Christ. "If," said he, "every tile on every house-roof at Worms were a devil, yet still I would go."

Many years afterwards, when the great reformer was drawing near to life's evening, he alluded to the emotions of exultant joy which he experienced at that hour, saying to his friends, "I felt no fear. God can give marvellous boldness. If the same thing had happened now, instead of then, I am not sure that I should feel such extraordinary liberty and exultation."

Note 7, page 61.

"He is pouring forth his troubled soul
　In sighs, and tears, and prayer."

It was even said of Luther's Divine Master, "It pleased the Father to bruise Him." And so, in a different sense, and for a widely different end, it may be said of the servant. One of the most affecting historical documents in existence is that which records his mental agony under a temporary sense of Divine desertion, as the hour drew near for his introduction to the Diet. His friends, who were waiting for his reappearance, outside the door of his closet, heard his earnest, agonising pleadings with his God and Father. For awhile a horror of thick darkness seems to have veiled the Mercy-seat. "O God!" he pleaded; "O God! Oh, Thou, my God! help me against all the wisdom of this world. Do this, I beseech Thee! Thou *shouldst* do this; . . . . by Thine own mighty power! . . . . The work is not mine, but Thine. I have no business here. . . . . I have nothing to contend for with these great men of the world! I would gladly pass my days in happiness and peace. But the cause is Thine . . . and it is righteous and everlasting! O Lord, help me! O, faithful and unchangeable God! I lean not upon man. It were vain! Whatever is of man is tottering; whatever proceeds from him must fall! My God! my God! Dost not Thou hear? My God! Art Thou no longer living? Nay, Thou canst not die! Thou dost but hide Thyself. Thou hast chosen me for this work. I know it! . . . Therefore, O God, accomplish Thine own will! Forsake me not, for the sake of Thy well-beloved Son, Jesus Christ, my defence, my buckler, and my stronghold!"

Then, after a moment of silent struggle, Luther continued:—"O Lord! where art Thou? . . . My God! where art Thou? . . . Come, I pray Thee; I am ready! . . . Behold me prepared to lay down my life for Thy truth! . . . suffering like a lamb! For the cause is holy. It is Thine own! . . . I will not let Thee go!

No, nor yet for all eternity! And though the world should
be thronged with devils, and though this body, which is the
work of Thine hands, should be cast forth, trodden under
foot, cut in pieces . . . consumed to ashes . . . MY
SOUL IS THINE! Yes! I have Thine own Word to assure
me of it. My soul belongs to Thee, and will abide with
Thee for ever! Amen! O God, send help! . . . Amen!"

See D'Aubigné's *History of the Reformation*, Eng. trans.,
vol. ii. page 289. See also Michelet's *Life of Luther.*

Merle D'Aubigné says that this prayer may be originally
found " dans le Recueil des Pièces relative à la comparation
de Luther, à Worms, sous le numero 16 ; au milieu de ' Sauf-
conduits,' et d'autres documents de ce genre."

NOTE 8, page 61.

" But he knows the Angel's ' Secret Name,'
And will not be denied."

Genesis, xxii. 26-29.

NOTE 9, page 63.

" The hour hath struck, and at its call
He rises up from prayer."

" Four o'clock arrived. The marshal of the empire appeared. Luther prepared to set out. God had heard his
prayer: he was calm when he quitted the hotel."— D'AU-
BIGNÉ.

NOTE 10, page 64.

" From the banks of yellow Tyber,
    From Danube's moaning river,
    From Weser, Elbe, and Vistula,
    And flowery Guadalquiver."

" And now the doors of the hall were thrown open. Luther entered; and many who constituted no part of the Diet gained admission with him. Never had any man appeared before so august an assembly."— D'AUBIGNÉ.

NOTE 11, page 64.

" The Empire's seven Electors."

Only six of the seven electors of the empire were present on this occasion.

NOTE 12, page 65.

" And the cloud across the anxious brow
    Of noble Saxony."

Frederick, surnamed the Wise, Elector of Saxony, was Luther's dear friend. It is a remarkable fact that they never met, face to face, till this hour; and, it is believed, never afterwards, till they met in heaven. The Duke of Alva, afterwards so famous (or rather so *infamous*) in the history of Protestantism, and his two sons, were present.

Note 13, page 66.

" My Kaiser!—here I take my stand,
God helping me!—Amen!"

" Hier stehe Ich!   Ich kan nicht anders.
Gott helfe mir!   Amen!"

Note 14, page 70.

" And the echo to the wrath of man
Is heard in songs of praise."

" Surely the wrath of man shall praise thee; and the remainder of wrath shalt thou restrain."— Psalm lxxvi. 10.

LAY OF THE WARTBURG.

"Sint Scripturæ quæ deliciæ meæ! Nec decipior in eis,
nec decipiam ex eis."—Augustine.

THERE was mourning on the banks of Elbe,

In the laughing month of May;

In town and hamlet, hall and cot,

Were sorrow and dismay.

There were boding sighs, and childlike tears,

By strong men freely shed;

And broken words—"Let foes beware—

Kaiser or Pope—if they but dare

To crush one single, honour'd hair

Upon that freeborn head!

" We care not for tiara crowns,

    Nor royal miniver !

The Saxon hath his coat of mail,

    And steed, and knightly spur !

We care not for the golden keys ;

    We have our iron fist ;

And thousand voices shall demand

The birthright of the Fatherland,

If Rome dare lay her crimson'd hand

    On Truth's evangelist."

There are haughty questionings and frowns,

    In proud, imperial hall ;

There was jubilee in Vatican,

    And on the Quirinal ;

And the ruddy wine-cup brimmeth o'er

    At many a festal board,

Because Rome dreams her stubborn foe

Hath pluck'd the arrow from his bow,

    And sheathed his daring sword.

There kneels an unknown captive Knight
  In a solitary tower ;
And he rises up to trim his lamp
  At evening's shadowy hour.
The dark pine-forests wave beneath,
  With hollow, troublous sighs ;
And the old oaks gather up the sound,
And send the moaning cadence round,
  And the ivied tower replies.

A soldier of a mighty King
  To Him his knee hath bow'd,
And the service of a duteous Knight
  Most loyally hath vow'd ; —
'Twas He who gave the hand its sword,
  And gave the breast its shield ; —
A King whose foemen he hath braved,
And glorious banner sternly waved
  In many a battle-field !

G

I ween men thought it strange to see
   Such stalwart cavalier,
(With hilted sword, and casque, and plume,
   And all a bold knight's gear),
With studious brow, so lined with thought,
   And introverted eye,
And hand endow'd with clerkly skill,
Guiding with energetic will
The movements of a vigorous quill,
   As hour by hour rolled by.

Now swept he royal David's harp
   With firm, yet reverent hand,
Making it vocal with the words
   Of his own Fatherland ;[1] —
Now bade the Saxon's mother-tongue
   Proclaim, in household word,
The high and holy doctrines taught,
And glorious deeds of wonder wrought,
   By David's King and Lord.

The summer came, with gifts to earth —

    Sunshine and balmy shower —

Lengthening the ivy's muffling clasp

    Around the ancient tower ;

And Autumn, with her ripening suns,

    Storm-clouds, and ruddy gleams,

And mellow fruits, and garnered sheaves,

And sobbing winds, and rustling leaves,

    And flashing mountain-streams.

" Rise up, Sir Knight ! I ween thy brow,

    With hard soul-conflicts lined,

Will throb less hurriedly if fann'd

    By the cool forest-wind.

Come forth, and join the jovial troop

    Who rise, with morrow's dawn,

And leave the Wartburg's gloomy tower,

The breezy woodland-paths to scour,

    With hawk, and hound, and horn !" [2]

*   *   *   *

*   *   *

The jasper portals of the morn
  In silence backward roll'd,
And pour'd upon the waking earth
  A flood of molten gold.
The old oak doors in Wartburg tower
  Creak'd open, one by one ;
The spurs are clattering in the yard,
The heavy fastenings are unbarr'd,
  And the gates are backward thrown.

There were noble knights and sturdy squires,
  With plumes and sheathèd swords ;
There were jägers, with their winding horns,
  And jests and wrangling words.

The Landgraf, with his massive curb,
    Bridled his chafing steed ;
And the spicy " stirrup-cup " went round,
And horse and rider, hawk and hound,
    The castle-gate have freed.

'Twas not to marshal feats of arms
    That the shrill clarion blew,
But for the peaceful forest-chase—
    The wild-wood *rendezvous!*
And many a noble stag who browsed,
    That morn, in antler'd pride,
Sobb'd out his life on upland fell,
Or stood at bay in forest dell,
Ere the loud bugle's winding swell
    Sounded at eventide.

What rider and what gallant steed
    Were foremost in the chase,

And which excell'd in strength or skill,
   'Twere tedious to retrace.
Down forest-glades—o'er upland steeps—
   They strove with will and might;
And the solemn wild-wood rang with glee,
As shouted, loud and merrily—
   All—save the Wartburg Knight!

They marvell'd what might be his crest,
   And what his pedigree;
And yet they read upon his brow
   Truth, Trust, and Loyalty!—
A hand unused to rein a steed,
   Or wear a jewell'd ring,
And yet an eye whose fire might grace
The loftiest line, the proudest race,
With a bold sparkle that might face
   Kaiser, or Pope, or King!

'Twas plain to see that soul like his
  Breathed not her native air,
Amid the death-wail and the shout,
  The tumult and the glare.
Leagued with the strong against the weak,
  He sighed, and stood apart.
Oh ! he could well-nigh bare his breast,
Between oppressor and oppressed,
  And hug the bitter dart.

When the poor quarry wounded sank,
  And triumph-shouts rose high,
He only saw, of sin and grief,
  The symboled mystery.
And big tears, down his manly cheek,
  In heavy drops would roll :
" Alas !" he sighed; " behold the way
Sin's Antichrist doth still waylay,
And hunt his feeble, trembling prey,
  The deathless human soul !"

Anon, he spied a leveret
    Entangled in a snare ;
And then he brake the subtle toils,
    And freed the trembling hare.
He wrapped her softly in his cloak,
    With strangely gentle hands ;
" Thus would I snatch from sin's control,
Thus would I, in love's mantle roll
(Heaven grant me grace !) the fettered soul,
    And crush Rome's deadly bands !"

There were who list the strange Knight's words,
    And stopped, and looked aghast ;
But others gave their steeds the spur,
    And bounded fleetly past :
And others sent a jovial laugh
    Adown the forest aisle ;
But the Landgraf gave his plume a toss,
And with young Johann of the Schloss[3]
    Exchanged a conscious smile.

Yet neither Johann of the Schloss,

   Nor yet the Landgraf guessed,

What labouring thoughts are wrestling hard

   Within that true Knight's breast.

His soul is gathering up her strength,

   His Master's cross to bear ;

In weakness — taking hold of might,

In darkness — stretching forth to light,

Watching for morning through the night,

   In the energy of prayer.

He is learning how his Lord can work

   Without his feeble aid ;

How, for Christ's glory, man's renown

   Must choose the valley's shade.

He is hurried from the battle-field,

   And taught to sheathe *his* sword,

For one brief space — one restless span,

That the great work his voice began,

Be not achieved by might of man,

   But by the *Spirit's Word.*

Less need for Luther's rousing voice,
   By altar and by hearth,
Soon as the Gospel's silver trump
   Christ's message soundeth forth !
Less need that Luther's urn of clay
   Truth's precious drops should pour,
Soon as the living waters glide,
Freely and full in native tide,
   By cot and cabin door.

When, from the Wartburg's Patmos shades,
   Christ's own true Knight shall come,
With the Saxon's Bible in his hand,
   For the Saxon's hearth and home ;
When God's own Gospel shall declare
   The strength of man as vain,
The Spirit's sword of heavenly might
Shall carve Truth's pathway through the fight,
And out of darkness bringing light,
   The Lord alone shall reign !

NOTES.

———

Note 1, page 82.

" Now swept he royal David's harp
With firm, yet reverent hand,
Making it vocal with the words
Of his own Fatherland," &c.

Luther's captivity in the Wartburg was an interval from
personal action replete with the most important results
to the dawning Reformation. " Before this time," writes
Merle D'Aubigné, " Luther had translated some fragments
of the Holy Scriptures. . . . These earlier essays had
been eagerly bought up, and had awakened a general
demand for more; and this desire on the part of the people
was regarded by Luther as a call from God. He resolved
to meet it. He was now a captive, enclosed within lofty
walls; but what of that? He wanted this time of leisure to
render the Word of God into the language of his nation.
Soon shall we see that *Word* descending with him from the
Wartburg, circulating among the families of Germany, and
enriching them with spiritual treasure, hitherto shut up
within the hearts of a few pious persons. . . . Thence-

forth the Reformation was no longer in the hands of the
Reformer. The BIBLE was brought forward, and Luther
held a secondary place. The Reformer placed the Book in
the hands of the people; thenceforth each might hear God
Himself speaking to him: and as for Luther, he mingled in
the crowd, placing himself among those who came to draw
from the common fountain of light and life."— *English
Translation*, vol. iii. p. 39.

NOTE 2, page 83.

" Rise up, Sir Knight," &c.

" The life of the Doctor of Wittenberg, in his assumed
character of Knight, had indeed, at times, a something
about it truly theological.   One day there was a grand
preparation for a hunting party, and Luther, whose health
was suffering from unwonted bodily inaction, was invited to
join the chase.   " The snares were made ready, the fortress
gates thrown open, the dogs let loose.   The huntsmen were
in high spirits; the dogs scoured the hills, driving the
hares from the brushwood.   But as the tumult swelled
around him, *the Knight George* (Luther's disguised name),
motionless in the midst of it, felt his soul fill with
solemn thoughts.   Looking around him, his heart heaved
with sorrow.   ' Is not this,' said he, ' the very picture of the
Devil, setting his dogs, the bishops, those messengers of
Antichrist, to hunt down poor souls?'   A young leveret
had been snared; and Luther, rejoicing to liberate it,
wrapped it in his mantle, and deposited it in the midst of a
thicket.   But scarcely had he left the spot when the dogs
scented it, and killed it.   Drawn to the place by its cry,

Luther uttered an exclamation of grief:—'O Pope! and thou too, O Satan! it is thus that ye would compass the destruction of the souls that have been seemingly rescued from death!'"— D'AUBIGNÉ, vol. iii. p. 20.

NOTE 3, page 88.

"And with young Johann of the Schloss."

Johann von Berlepsch was Provost of the Wartburg during Luther's imprisonment there.

THE HERMIT OF LIVRY.

A PAGE FROM FRENCH HISTORY OF THE FIFTEENTH CENTURY.

PART I.

> " For the most loved are they
> Of whom Fame speaks not, with her clarion voice,
> In regal halls.   The shades o'erhang their way;
> The vale, with its deep fountains, is their choice.
> .   .   .   .   And gentle hearts rejoice
> Around their steps."   FELICIA HEMANS.

Within an ancient forest lone,

 Beside a tinkling well,

An Eremite, long years agone,

 Had scooped his little cell.

With fragrant shootings of the pine

 He strewed the rock-hewn floor ;

And trained the briery eglantine
    On either side the door.

He wove his couch with ozier wands,
    And laid his bed with moss ;
And at its foot, with pious hands,
    He hung his beechen cross.

And when his vesper psalm was sung,
    At balmy close of day,
Within its cresset chain he hung
    His little lamp of clay.

No worldling's footstep dare disturb
    His sweet and placid hours ;
Conning, perchance, some healing herb,
    Or watering his flowers.

The huntsman, with a bugle blast,
    Recalled the eager hound,

Long ere the chestnut shades were passed
    Which girt that cell around.

But helpless things, and wan, and weak,
    And sorrowful, and poor,
Knew well which narrow path to seek,
    To reach the hermit's door.

The wounded hare would fearless come,
    And drink beside his well ;
The squirrel coved his winter home
    Within his mossy cell.

And forest birds of shyest mood
    Would flutter in and out ;
And share his scanty dole of food,
    Without a fear or doubt.

But though, for every mortal ill,
    He mixed the balmy cup,

When wounded spirits craved his skill,
With all his pity and goodwill,
  He could not bind them up.

He could not give to soul's afaint
  The manna of the word ;
He loved the legendary saint,
  Yet hardly knew his Lord.

He conned his missal o'er and o'er,
  And rung its changes round ;
But of the Gospel's holy lore
  He scarcely knew the sound.

But He who heals the blind and halt,
  And breaks the captive's thrall,
Will soon, with larger trusts, exalt
  The faithful in the small.

It was the balmy month of May ;
And from his mossy bed
The hermit rose at break of day,
Just as the mavis on the spray
His matin hymn had said ;

Just as a slanting sunbeam stole
Adown the forest aisle,
And fretted branch, and hoary bole,
Grew ruddy with its smile ;

Just as the lily's silver bell
By morn's first breeze was shaken ;
Just as the wild doe at the well
Her morning thirst had slaken.

And when his missal's sweetest lay
Had glided off his lip,
The hermit girt his hodden grey,
And took his staff and scrip.

He took his failing cruise of oil,
  And eke his wallet scant,
To sue for alms, with patient toil,
  A lowly mendicant.

He slowly trod, with sandaled feet,
  The forest's dappled floor,
Singing his " *Paternosters* " sweet,
  And "*Aves*,"—o'er and o'er.

God's earth beneath — God's sky above,
  Throbbed as with life and light ;
And yet the wondrous name of Love
  He could not read aright.

And as his spirit pondered o'er
  The viewless and the seen,
And listened to that river's roar
  Which darkly flows between,

His poor heart shivered on its bank,

And heard the billows toss,

But saw no barque, no bridge, no plank,

To bear him safe across.

PART II.

The lily's silver bell had tolled
   The sunset's dewy hour,
And holy Vespertide had rolled
Its fulgent waves of molten gold
   Adown the forest bower;

Filling each amber cup and bell,—
   Gilding each bough and shaft,—
Turning to chrysolite the well
   At which the wild doe quaffed.

The little birds, with look askant,
   Expect their wonted store;
The squirrel, pert and petulant,
   Is chafing at the door.

He comes! Oh gentle Eremite,
  With staff, and cross, and scrip;
What means that smile of heavenly light
  Which trembles on thy lip?

Say, hast thou scanned, like one of yore,
  A shining heavenward road,
Up which the sinful and the poor
  May climb direct to God?

Down which angelic pinions move,
  Bearing good gifts to men,
And answering messages of love
  Return to heaven again?

Perchance thy hands, with eager haste,
  This day have grasped a dole,
Sweeter than honey to the taste,
Dearer than well-spring in the waste,
  To the poor fainting soul.

The staff and scrip aside are laid ;
   The little lamp is trimmed ;
The evening psalm is softly said ;
The " *Paternoster*" prayer is prayed,
   But not one " *Ave*" hymned.

And when, within his coved cell,
   The squirrel slept serene,
And the pale lamp-light softly fell
   Upon the quiet scene ;

It lit the placid brow of age,
   All reverently bent
Over the glorious Gospel page
   Of Christ's NEW TESTAMENT.

The "*Compline*" hour unheeded went ;
   The "*Nocturn*" watch is gone ;
And still that reverent brow is bent,
   And still that eye reads on ;

Beholding where the Saviour dwelt,
  Dwelling with Him, in thought;
Kneeling, in spirit, where He knelt,
  And listening when He taught;

Launching upon the midnight sea,
  By the storm-pinion swept;
Talking with Christ at Bethany,
  And weeping when He wept;

Rising with Mary when she heard
  That her dear Lord was come;
Hearkening the resurrection word
  Of victory o'er the tomb;

Slow following to the Judgment-hall,
  With bitter tears—yet sweet;
Tasting the wormwood and the gall,
  Kissing the wounded feet;

Searching the dark tomb for the Dead ;

    Hailing the shining vision ;

And heeding what the angel said,—

    " *He is not here—but risen!*"

Meeting at Galilee the Christ ;

    Noting each gracious word ;

And, with the dear Evangelist,

    Exclaiming, " 'Tis the Lord !"

Looking up steadfastly on high,

    The while his Lord ascends,

And grasping the peace-legacy

    Of Jesus to His " friends !"

And ere the cresset lamp burned dull,

    And ere night's shadows part,

The Sun of Righteousness rose full

    On his rejoicing heart.

Now hath he cordials for the faint
　　They never found before ;
Medicines for every woe and plaint,
　　And riches for the poor.

For wounded hearts, and sick, and sad,
　　He hath a healing balm ;
And for the whole, and young, and glad,
　　A sweet thanksgiving psalm.

The poor dumb creatures of the grove
　　His bounty still partake ;
He loved them with a better love,
　　For his dear Saviour's sake.

But most he loved the sinner's soul,
　　And yearned to publish round,
The saving grace which made *him* whole,
　　The heaven his heart had found.

So, with the name of Christ, his Lord,
    Engraven on his lip,
Goes forth a preacher of the Word,
    With Bible, staff, and scrip ;

Receiving from the cold and stern
    The bitter herbs of strife ;
And giving back, in sweet return,
    The heavenly Bread of life.

PART III.

The choristers, with hurried glee,
 Have chaunted the last psalm,
And the great bell swingeth heavily
 In the tower of Notre Dame!

And a city's life-blood, at the sound,
 Stops with a sudden start;
And then with strong convulsive bound,
Flows to one common central ground,
 As to its throbbing heart.

Through a hundred alleys, dark and deep,
 The black tide rushes on,
With roar, and swirl, and maddened leap,
 At the great bell's heavy tone.

The cripple seizes on his crutch,

   And staggers through the throng ;

The squalid Mother in her clutch,

   Drags the scared child along.

The courtier clasps his baldrick bright

   O'er robe of miniver ;

The hero from his hundredth fight

   Puts on his gilded spur.

The mitred Bishop mounts his mule,

   In rich caparison ;

The theologian quits his school,

   In the halls of the Sorbonne.

The bridegroom leaves the feast and song ;

   The monk his "Ave" psalm ;

All—all to swell that surging throng,

   In the square of Notre Dame ;

Where the ancient dial points the hour,
     As with the wand of death :
And the great bell swingeth in the tower,
     And the people yell beneath ;

All gazing, with the demon smile
     Of fratricidal Cain,
Upon a gloomy funeral pile,
     A stake, a torch, a chain !

And on the left, and on the right,
     A thousand tongues exclaim,
" Bring forth the impious Eremite,
     To death, and woe, and shame !"

And now a grim procession steers
     Its snake-like course along ;
With monks, and priests, and halberdiers,
Carving a pathway with their spears,
     Amidst the panting throng.

Who *is* he : with that soft, mild eye,

    So dulled by prison thrall :

And that firm step of courage high,

And look of patient constancy,

    No terrors can appal ?

Who is he ?   Ask the poor and low ;

    And ask the wan and sick ;

And ask the helpless if *they* know

    The impious heretic.

And ask the small birds of the air

    Who shared his scanty dole ;

And ask the lithe and frisking hare

    His gentle hands made whole.

And ask the sinful of his skill,

    And let the saved repeat,

How beautiful upon the hill,

    Were once those fettered feet !

But the great bell swayeth to and fro,
  In the tower of Notre Dame ;
And heavily, and harsh, and slow,
  They chaunt the funeral psalm.

He heareth not the dolorous hymn,
  Nor heeds the rush and roar ;
He is walking by a river's brim,
And listening to the Seraphim
  Upon the farther shore.

He is standing by a river's bank,
  But sees no billows toss ;
And asks no barque, no bridge, no plank,
  To bear him safe across.

For he sees a chariot as of fire,
  With wheels of scorching flame ;
And then the angel-song grew nigher,
  And Jesus quickly came.

Thus rose he to the realms of bliss,

   Glorious — yet silently ;

And left no name on earth but this —

   " THE HERMIT OF LIVRY."

Yet in the courts of light and love

   His name is brightly graven ;

His praise is registered above,

   His record is in heaven.

SCRIPTURE LYRICS.

THE BOY OF LYSTRA.

PART I.

" And that from a child thou hast known the Holy
Scriptures."— 2 *Tim.* iii. 15.

THE morning breeze was sighing
   O'er Lystra's arid plain ;
And slowly waved the dark stone pine,
And fanned the clusters of the vine,
   And stirred the rustling grain.
An orient streak was paling
   The rising matin star ;
They said it was the golden fringe
   Of bright Apollo's car !

And there be warbling voices,
   In dreamy fall and swell,

From maidens, bearing empty urns
   Adown the olive dell ;
And singing, as they pass along,
The snatches of a choral song
   To the Naiad of the well.

And from the city portal
   Rolls forth a pæan sound,
From white-robed priests with flowing hair
   In golden fillets bound ;
Chaunting the mighty triumphs
   Of Lystra's sceptred Jove ;
While to his colonnaded fane,
Timing their footsteps to the strain,
   In stately file they move.

But hush ! Whence steals that warbling,
   So soft and liquid clear ?
Sure, never muse from Phocian Mount,
Nor nymph from Ida's sweetest fount,
   Hath tuned that dulcimer !

Three voices!—*one*,—though chastened
    By time, still led the hymn :
But *one* might e'en have caught its tone
    From far-off Seraphim !
And *one*,—the ringing treble,
    As of some sweet-voiced boy,
Whose heart was full of echo-haunts
    For notes of love and joy !

Their speech is of a country
    Beyond the purple hills ;
Nor wafted by Thessalian breeze,
Nor taught by fair Pierides,
    Beside Castalian rills.
They sang like Amram's daughter
    Beside dark Egypt's sea :
They sang as royal David sung,
The while his cunning hand he flung
    O'er harp and psaltery.

Though the Boy's accent hinted
   Of Hellas' classic prime,
And of a Grecian Father's tongue,
   And fair Ægean clime.

'Twas beautiful,—beholding
   Those Hebrew mothers sweet,
And that high-browed and earnest youth,
Who listened to the words of truth,
   Reclining at their feet;
Spell-fastened by a Volume,
   Unrolled upon his knee;
—The pæan chorus rose on high,
Nor flushed his cheek, nor fired his eye,
And maidens, from the well, went by,
   Nor stirred his reverie.

What unseen treasure hideth
   Within that ancient scroll?

No graceful lore seems lettered there,
In fair Hellenic character,
  To trance his heaven-born soul.
His thoughts are in that country,
  Beyond the purple hills :
A land of showers and fruitful vales,
Of balmy dews and spicy gales,
  Of fountains and of rills.
With kindling eye he questions
  The dim and faded scroll :
Striving to weave, midst many a sigh,
The golden threads of prophecy,
With holy type and promise high,
  In one harmonious whole.

He reads of sceptred Judah :
  Of Jessie's royal stem :
He readeth of a Branch of might,
A Star to rise on Israel's night,
A throne of everlasting light,
  A glorious Diadem !

When prostrate kings shall worship,

   And subject tribes shall fear ;

And Gentile nations shall behold,

And bring their incense and their gold,

   And far-off sons draw near;

The waste shall bud like Eden,

   And desert places bloom:

Then spake the Boy, with glistening eyes,

" Oh *when* shall Judah's Sceptre rise ?

When dawn the Star on Israel's skies ?

   When shall the kingdom come ?

" So long ! so long, my Mother !

   Why tarrieth He so late ?"

" My son, the while He seems to stay,

He girdeth on His bright array ;

His chariot wheels are on the way : —

   Blessed are they who wait !"

PART II.

" The gods are come down to us in the likeness of men."—
Acts, xiv. 2.

Thrice blest were they who waited

    The day-spring from on high ;

Blest were they, through the shades of night,

Blest at the dawning of the light,

And blessed with blessings kept in sight

    By Faith's unwearied eye.

According as it listeth

    So blows the wind of heaven ;

According to appointed hour,

As drops the dew on upturned flower,

    So was the blessing given.

Yet many a breeze of morning
  Still sighed o'er Lystra's plain,
And murmured in the dark stone pines,
And shook the ripe fruits from the vines,
  And swept the golden grain.
Still, at the city portal,
  The crippled beggar lay ;
And still in purple robe, swept by
The rich man with averted eye,
  Exultant on his way.
And still, at dewy morning,
  And still at evening's calm,
Awoke the same sweet symphony
From dulcet harp, and psaltery,
And woke those Hebrew voices three,
  Chaunting the holy psalm.

But look !   Whence come those Strangers
  Who stand at Lystra's gate ?

The one, with calm, benignant face,

With lofty brow and winning grace,

Moves forward with a stately pace,

    As of no mean estate.

And one, of meaner stature,

    Treads firm in hidden might.

Sure, none could ever search that eye

Of strong concentered energy,

    And e'er forget its light.

That brow — how firm! how earnest!

    That look — how keen, yet mild!

That changing cheek, whose rapid glow

Speaks of quick feelings, free to flow

Forth to all human hearts below,

    Down to each lisping child!

A heart whose boundless yearnings

    Encompass land and sea.

Poor cripple! will he pass *thee* by?

Think'st thou he notes thy whispered sigh?

Perchance if thou, in faith, draw nigh,

    He hath an alms for thee.

There rung a wild, strange chorus
   That hour, through Lystra's street.
Torches were tossing in the air,
Flamens rushed by with frenzied glare,
And women, with unbraided hair,
   Loose zones, and tinkling feet.
With triumph-shout and pæan
   The stifling air was rent :
" The gods revisit earth again ;
Hail, Jove ! great king of gods and men !
   Hail, Hermes, eloquent !
Hail to the son of Chronos !
   Hail to the Pleiad-born !
The gods descend with healing art,
The lame man leapeth as a hart,
Woes of the iron age depart ; —
   Hail to earth's golden morn !
Garland the milk-white heifer !
   Bring rams with curving horn !
Hail to old Saturn's mighty son,
The thunderer of the ivory throne !
   Hail to the Pleiad-born !"

The glittering axe is lifted,

   The milk-white victim stands,

Fondling the hand prepared to slay,

And in her mild, unconscious play,

   Cropping her flowery bands.

The flashing steel, uplifted,

   Is shimmering in the light :

" *Hold!*" speaks a voice, at whose command

The axe reels in the flamen's hand,

And men in mute inquiry stand,

   Controlled by viewless might.

" We be not gods, but mortals ;

   With passions like your own.

We come to turn your lightened eyes

From idol rite and sacrifice,

   To serve one God alone.

One living God! Oh, Lystrians !

   The Heaven of heavens is His :

He framed it by His own decree,

He made the earth, the sky, the sea,

And all that therein is.

Each season is his witness,

   That all He doth is good :

He gives the sunshine and the rain,

The fruitful field, the laughing plain,

   The gladness and the food !"

Oh, there were high debatings,

   That eve, in Lystra's street.

" Strange !—that with passions like our own,

Men scorn the thyrsis and the crown,

And glory, homage, all cast down,

   As at a master's feet !

An unseen Lord and Master :

   Beneath whose wondrous sway

Olympian gods stand disarrayed,

Discrowned, dethroned,— a myth, a shade ;

And poets' tuneful dreamings fade,

   Like morning mists, away !"

PART III.

"And that, from a child, thou hast known the Holy Scriptures, which are able to make thee wise unto salvation; through faith which is in Christ Jesus."—2 *Tim.* iii. 15.

REST for the weary footstep !

 Sleep for the troubled eye !

Dews for faint flower and drooping bough!

Soft smoothings for the furrowed brow !—

Oh night, how angel-like art thou !

 How blest thy lullaby !

The drowsy breeze of summer

 Scarce sighs its interlude.

So hushed is every viewless string,

You almost hear the turtle's wing

 Stir o'er her nestled brood ;

And the sweet Naiad of the spring,

In tinkling whispers answering

　　The Dryad of the wood.

Calm o'er the slumbering city

　　The steady planets roll ;

And Pleiads their sweet influence pour,

As if a pitying love they bore

　　For man's bewildered soul.

What means that light forthshining

　　So steadily, yet pale,

Down from one casement's latticed height ?

Too earthward for a planet's light,

And yet too pure, too mild, too slight,

　　For earthly festival !

Amidst that dreaming city,

　　None heed its feeble spark :

But angel watchers know the place,
And, poised on viewless wings, they trace
The shinings of the lamp of grace
    Within this household ark.

What see they here to rivet
    Such fixed, ecstatic gaze ?
A single lamp, of flickering strength,
A scroll, in all its breadth and length,
    Unroll'd beneath its rays.
A great Apostle's finger
    Is moving o'er that scroll ;
And letters dim shine forth like gold,
And shades obscure are backward roll'd,
And dark enigmas straight unfold
    Before his list'ners' soul.

'Twas beautiful to witness
    Those Hebrew mothers twain.

With folded hands and heavenward eye,
Clasping the message from on high,
Like autumn flowers, athirst and dry,
  Drinking the latter rain.

And thou, oh, young disciple !
  The child of faith and prayer ;
What is it sweeps thy radiant brow
With something like the cypress bough,
As if a trailing cloud, e'en now,
  Had cast its shadow there ?
Why doth thy yearning spirit
  Still wander down the scroll ?
Still turning back to " Jesse's Stem,"
And sceptred Judah's diadem,
  Like needle to the pole ?

Ah ! there be low, soft breathings,
  Thy touch not yet hath stirred,

In the grand harp of prophecy ;
And thy young hand hath passed these by,
  Unheeded and unheard.
Now bend thine ear to listen :
  And faith shall plume her wing,
And love, in holy reverence stand,
The while the great Apostle's hand
  Shall wake the plaintive string.

Behold, thine own Messiah,
  To work redemption's plan,
Must lay the regal vesture by,
And come " in great humility "—
  " *Emmanuel — God with man !*"
Behold the " Man of sorrows !"
  The lowly Virgin-born !
" Despised," " rejected," counted base,
And hiding not His smitten face
  " From spitting and from scorn !"

Behold the " bruised "—the " wounded !"—

  " The wormwood and the gall !"—

Behold the " Lamb to slaughter led,"

The victim, on whose dying head

    Were laid the sins of all !

" Accounted with transgressors ; "

    " Afflicted "—scorn'd—" abhorred ! "—

Then spake the youth, with reverent brow,

" Messiah !—Christ !—I know Thee now !—

  Jesus !—my God !—my Lord !

I know Thee in Thy sorrow—

    Thine agony—Thy grief !

Love's wondrous heights I strain to span :

Oh, Son of God !—Oh, Son of Man !—

    Help Thou mine unbelief !

" Death could not break Thy sceptre :

    Thy kingdom *yet* shall come ;

And Gentile nations shall bow down,

And Israel's contrite sons shall own

Their Saviour's cross — their Ruler's crown —

And come, with singing, home!"

THE BROTHERS.

"By faith, Abel offered unto God a more excellent sacrifice than Cain; by which he obtained witness that he was righteous; God testifying of his gifts: and by it he, being dead, yet speaketh."—*Heb.* xi. 4.

THOUGH the opal gates of Eden

    Be for ever shut and barr'd;

Though to heaven, on mournful pinion,

    Back return'd the Angel-guard;

There was beauty in earth's ruins,

    Fragrance in her tangled bowers;

There was glory in the storm-cloud,

    And a star for midnight hours.

There was gladness in the sadness

   Of poor Eve, the while she smiled —

Smiled and wept, and sighed and ponder'd,

   O'er her first and new-born child :

Musing o'er her gotten treasure ;

   Striving, in her infant's face,

To decipher holy meanings —

   Hidden blessings — germs of grace !

·' Have I gotten from Jehovah

   The true, promised Seed ?" she said ;

" Sorely bruised my heel the serpent,

   But my Seed shall bruise his head."

Sometimes heavenward — sometimes childward —

   Her sweet, pensive brow she turn'd —

Broken melodies soft chanting,

   Which in Edenland she learn'd !

Soon to sadness turn'd all gladness,
 As the seasons swiftly flew,
And the firstling of her cradle
 On to wilful boyhood grew.

One by one, bright hopes have wither'd —
 One by one, dark fears unfold :
Sin hath canker'd Eve's young rosebud —
 Sin hath changed to dross her gold !

Proud and restless was his bearing,
 Passionate his eye, and wild ;
Strong in will, perverse, and froward —
 Such was Adam's first-born child.

Who shall say what boding anguish
 Planted in Eve's breast the thorn,
When she wove the osier cradle
 For her little second-born ?

Who shall say what early breathings
    Of the dove-like Spirit stole,
In the freshness of life's morning,
    O'er young Abel's quicken'd soul?

Child of Adam, earth-born, carnal,
    Offspring of a sinful race ;
Son of wrath — yet heir of glory,
    Born of God — a child of grace !

Now, perchance, he loved to commune
    With his Mother, hand in hand,
Listening to her holy stories
    Of the vanish'd Edenland ; —

Of the flowers that never wither'd,
    Of the fruits that ne'er decay'd,
Of the glory of the mountain,
    And the music of the glade ; —

Of the holy angel-voices,

   Of the harpings heard from heaven,

Of sweet converse with Jehovah,

   In the cool and hush of even ;—

Of the hour of sin and darkness,

   Of the Cherub's flaming sword,

Of God's plighted grace, in promise —

   Paradise by Christ restored !

Now, perchance, his flock he folded

   On the soft and dewy mead,

Pondering o'er his father's teachings,

   Why the spotless lamb must bleed ;—

Why, upon Jehovah's altar,

   Blood of victim must be spilt,

Ere the rebel can be pardon'd,

   Ere the sinful wash'd from guilt !

Faith embraced the truth mysterious,
   Which the sign but dimly show'd ;
Looking onward, as it ponder'd,
   To the Holy Lamb of God.

Years have flown,—nor fail'd to ripen
   Fruits of life and seeds of death :—
Cain's hard heart grew harder, darker—
   Abel's grew " from faith to faith."

Elder Brother! wherefore flasheth
   Proud defiance in thine eyes,
As the holy hour approacheth
   For the evening sacrifice?

On the upland stand two altars,
   In the balmy sunset air ;
And the wood is set in order,
   And the Brothers twain stand there.

Abel owns himself a sinner,

   Needing the atoning blood ;

So he brings a spotless lambkin,

   At the bidding of his God.

Cain stood up, erect and haughty,

   And upon his altar heaped

Fruits of earth (a vain oblation !)

   His own hands had sown and reaped !

Can such offering, self-provided,

   Favour and acceptance find

With a holy God, who searcheth

   All the workings of man's mind ?

Cold upon the pile, unheeded,

   Cain's rejected offering lies ;

While a flood of heavenly glory

   Kindles Abel's sacrifice.

Upward, heavenward, thence ascending
    To the fount from whence it came,
Through the calm and perfumed ether,
    Rose the pure and holy flame.

Ah! what passions, fell and furious,
    Rush on Cain, in whelming flood,
Darken o'er his brow of hatred,
    And imbrue his hands in blood!

Turn we from the deed of darkness —
    Turn we from the crimson'd sod ;
Heavenward turn we, where the spirit
    Of the " righteous" mounts to God !

Where the gates of pearl flew open,
    And Archangels veiled their face,
As they list the " *new song*," chaunted
    By the first of mortal race.

And the Seraphs paused to hearken
　To the music of that Name,
By a ransom'd soul first utter'd :—
　" *Worthy—worthy is* THE LAMB !

" 'Twas His grace that brought me hither—
　'Twas His hand my victory won :
No man cometh to the Father,
　　But through merit of the Son.

" 'Twas the virtue of His life-blood *
　Wash'd my guilty soul from sin ;
'Twas the mention of His merits
　　Oped these gates, and let me in.

" 'Twas His Holy Spirit clothed me
　In this glorious robe of light :

* " The Lamb slain from the foundation of the world."—
Rev. xiii. 8.

'Tis His Righteousness approves me
  Righteous in the Father's sight!"

*   *   *   *   *   *   *

Who is this?—the scathed and branded,
  Scorning to repent and live;
Seeking rest—yet finding torment;—
  Harden'd, guilty, fugitive!

All who saw him shunn'd the slayer;
  On his hand they knew the stain;—
Mothers whisper'd to their children,
  In a warning voice—"*'Tis Cain!*"

"WARNED OF GOD."

HEBREWS, XI. 7.

FAIR rolled the rivers in rejoicing flow ;
  Bright fell the sunlight down on flowery glades ;
And summer winds, in pulses soft and low,
  Breathed trembling music 'mid the quivering shades.

The purple mountains 'gainst a cloudless sky,
  Undimmed by portent of foreshadowing mist,
Bore up, in strength, the vaulted canopy,
  Like moveless pillars of bright amethyst.

Earth sat at ease ! Her children up and down
  Paced restlessly ; or idly dreamed among
Her festal bowers ; or wove the nuptial crown ;
  Or led the mazy dance, with harp and song.

And man was beautiful! His brow still told
   Of primal glory, fading fast away;
The noble image of its Godlike mould
   Still lingered round the tenement of clay.

The giant stature, and the stately grace;
   The lofty mien, unbent by toil or time;
The glowing beauty of the upturned face.
   Still bore the impress of a type sublime.

Earth sat at ease! Sin's lethal bowl was crowned
   With poison flowers; and men drank deep and laughed,
And passed the cup, from hand to hand, around;
   And counted bitter sweet, the while they quaffed.

They heard not (for their ears were waxèd dull)
   The wailing dirge the morning stars then sang,
'Stead of creation's birthsong beautiful,
   With which the vaulted dome of heaven erst rang.

They see not (for their eyes are waxen dim)
  That the full measure of their sins runs o'er ;
The cup of wrath is foaming to its brim
  Which Justice stands, with outstretched hand, to pour.

But hark !   Amid the dim old woods is heard
  The clang of axe.   Then reeled the ancient oak ;
And the wild echoes of the hills are stirred
  With the sharp clangour of the hammer's stroke.

The mighty cedar shook his crashing boughs,
  And slowly bent to earth his lordly head ;
The lofty pines inclined their dusky brows,
  And balmy firs their resin tear-drops shed.

The ear of faith the gathering storm had heard ;
  The eye of faith had seen the uplifted rod ;
The work of faith was to obey God's word ;
  The hidden life of faith,—to " *walk with God.*"

Strong in their bands of sin, earth's son's deride

    The warning voice : and ask, with scornful lip,

" Where be the fountains of the whelming tide ?

    Where rolls the sea to float thy mighty ship ? "

But ever in the silence of the morn,

    And ever in the dewy hush of even,

The fragrant breath of sacrifice was borne

    Right upward to the glorious gates of heaven,

From one lone altar.   Singly and alone,

    It witnessed to a world's apostate shame.

The Lord of grace vouchsafes that spot to own

    Where two or three are gathered in His name.

Men little knew how long the rod was stayed,

    By the uplifted hands of mighty prayer ;

How long the hour of Justice was delayed,

    By virtue of the Love which pleaded there.

But man repented not ; and pitying Love
   Would lose all glory if she dare depress
The sceptre of God's justice ; or to move
   One pillar from His throne of righteousness.

Flee to the mountains — Death shall track thy flight !
   Hide in the valleys — Death arrives before !
Climb the wild peaks — cling to their craggy height :
   Death brooks no chain, no boundary, no shore !

Scale the tall tower — it crumbles into dust !
   Crouch with the trembling lion in his lair ;
Hie to the forest —'tis a worthless trust !
   Nest with the eagle — Death shall find thee there !

Launch the frail skiff—a crushed and shattered barque!
   Bind the firm raft — the black wave sucks it in !
Sinner ! Salvation owns but one true Ark :—
   One Saviour conquers Death by conquering Sin !

AN ARK SONG.

Oh how buoyantly she rideth
   O'er the heaving billows dark!
Oh how safe is he who hideth
   In Salvation's only Ark!

Though the sun and moon be shaded,
   Quenched be every planet's spark,
Every orb of light be faded,
   There is light within the Ark!

Though without be fear and quailing,
   Cries of wild despair: yet hark!
'Midst the tempest's moan and wailing,
   Holy anthems glad the Ark!

Though no hand her helm be guiding,
　　Though her course no compass mark,
Yet our Ship is safely riding,
　　Love is pilot of the Ark!

Though man's hopes have perished wholly,
　　Wrecked be every faithless barque,
For the trustful and the lowly
　　There is room within the Ark!

Saviour! ere the floods assailed us,
　　Ere each earthly lamp grew dark,
Ere the oil of gladness failed us,
　　We repaired to Thee,—our Ark!

A VOYAGE FROM TROAS TO NEAPOLIS.

A.D. 53.*

"Come over into Macedonia and help us."—*Acts*, xvi. 9.

" Now weigh the anchor, mariners!

And loose the flapping sail ;

And turn our galley's curving prow

Before the freshening gale.

O'er Ida's peak the paling stars

Are fading, one by one ;

And the Hours are harnessing the steeds

Of bright Latona's son.

The sparkle of his chariot wheels

Is glinting o'er the mountains ;

* The first introduction of the Gospel into Europe.

And leaping down, with argent sheen,

     Are Ida's many fountains.

And many a Naiad, fast asleep,

     He wakens with a kiss ;

And gilds Scamander's torpid stream,

     And ancient Simoïs.

And as he shakes his golden rein

     The flying axle glows,

And throws a smile across the isle

     Of classic Tenedos.

While, like a tide of chrysolite,

     From forth some orient font,

'Twixt glittering shores, down, downward pours

     The golden Hellespont !

And as he waves his fulgent locks

     O'er Lemnos, grey and cold,

Its shining coasts burst forth in light,

     As through a mist of gold.

On ! on ! and Ceres binds her sheaves,

     Midst Imbros' laughing bowers ;[1]

And ' sacred Samothrace' looks o'er [2]

The purple line of bending shore,

As when old Homer sang of yore,

 Of Troy's beleaguered towers.[3]

" *Io Apollo!*   On our helm

 Thy gold-tipt arrows shine ;

And the swelling sail hath caught the breeze,

And our idle rowers, at their ease,

 Along their bench recline.

Steer for the Hespern !—to the land

 Of the Pythian's mystic shrine ;

The laurel mount, and crystal fount,

 Dear to the tuneful Nine.

The land where a stainless robe of snow

 O'er Athos' shoulder falls :

The land of the Thunderer's ivory throne

 In bright Olympian halls !"

And so they steered ;—and so they clave

    The blue Ægean sea ;

And the chorus of the mariners

    Was shouted merrily ;

And the listening dolphins heard the song,

    And tossed the foam-bells round,

And played around the shallop's wake

    As if they loved the sound ;

And red libations were poured forth

    To fair Latona's son ;

And the helmsman turned the vessel's prow

    Right on for MACEDON.

Ha ! who be they ? those Strangers four,[*]

    Who joined not in the song ?

Who, when the foamy wine-cup poured

    Libations to the Pythian lord,

Sighed deep—and left the throng ?

    Sighed—as in pity and in love,

And moved the lip in prayer,

Heavenward! as if up paths of light

They communed with some God of might,

   Enthroned in glory there?

The seamen marvelled as they gazed

   Upon these wondrous men;

And marvelled at the strange, new name,

   (Unknown, unheard, till then),

Which dwelt, like music, on their lips,

   Or like some fragrant balm,

Transmuting sorrow into joy,

   And trouble into calm.

Such calm! They could not search its heights,

   Nor sound those depths of joy,

Which nought on earth could give, or take,

   Or 'minish, or alloy.

Well might they marvel, as they scanned

   That Hebrew stranger's* mien;

* St. Paul.

His eye of consecrated fire,
 So steadfast and serene !
The moulding of that spacious brow,
 Where Reason held firm seat,
Sublimed by Faith, was never wrought
 At proud Gamaliel's feet :
Nay !—nor in Attic portico,
 Nor academic grove ;
What subtle hand hath touched those lines
 Of tenderness and love ?

Steer for the Hespern ! He hath heard,
 Across the blue sea's foam,
A voice whose pleadings, strong and clear,
Are ringing in his thrilling ear,
 " *Come over !— help us !— come !*"[5]
From continent, and creek, and isle,
 From mount, and forest shade,
Resound the echoes of that cry,
 " Come over to our aid !"

'Twas like the pleading of the sick

    For one to make him whole ;

'Twas like the agonising wail

    Of some poor, dying soul !—

'Twas like the cry of trav'ller, lost

    On some dark mountain side,

Groping around a precipice,

    And shouting for a guide !—

'Twas like some captive's hollow groan,

    Lifting his fettered hands,

And calling, in his wild despair,

    For one to break his bands !—

'Twas like the sob of those who weep,

    And find no comforter !—

On, for the West,—the throbbing West !

    God hath a people there !

There,—in the city's crowded mart ;

    There,—in the forest lone ;

There,—in the palaces of kings,

    Christ shall a people own.

There,—in the craggy Alpine heights,
   Echoing the eagle's cry,
The Lord will choose His witnesses
   To live for Christ,—or die.

There,—by the Moldau and the Elbe,
   By field, and fell, and flood,
The martyrs' fiery car will leave
   Its glorious track in blood.

There,—in a northern Isle afar,—
   A land of brooks and rills,
Of fountains and of depths, that spring
   From valleys and from hills ;
A land whose sons are brave and free,
   Whose daughters, true and fair ;—
God's gracious purpose marks that Isle ;
   He hath much people there !

Away ! Away !   Again that cry ;
   Again that sobbing moan ;
" Come over !— over to our help !
   Come over to Macedon !"

Where Hæmus, girt with laurel zone,

    Lifts high his forehead bare ;

On for Philippi's mural towers :

    God hath a people *there!*

A man of stern and iron will,

    Welded 'mid sin and strife ;

Start not !—that gaoler's name is writ

    Within the book of life !

A woman, reaching forth her hands,

    Some viewless prize to win ;

In lowly faith, content to wait,

Meekly, at Truth's strong outer gate,

    Till Love should let her in !

On ! On !—The western hills grow red

    With the Day-god's parting kiss ;

And the shallop tosses high the spray,

As she drops her anchor in the bay

    Of old NEAPOLIS !

NOTES.

Note 1, page 154.

"   . . .   Ceres binds her sheaves
    Midst Imbros' laughing bowers."

Imbros was held sacred to Ceres.

Note 2, page 155.

" And ' sacred Samothrace' looks o'er
    The purple line of bending shore."

" Sacred Samothrace." — Samothracia was the " *Monte Santo* " of the ancient Greeks. It was the cradle of many heathen rites and superstitions; and was, moreover, a safe and inviolable asylum for criminals and fugitives.

Note 3, page 155.

" As when old Homer sang of yore
    Of Troy's beleaguered towers."

The author of *Eöthen* was much struck by the appearance of Samothrace, seen aloft over Imbros. He recollected how Jupiter is described in the *Iliad* as watching from thence the scene of the action before Troy. " Now I know," he says, " that Homer had passed along here; that this vision of Samothrace overtowering the nearer island was common to him and to me."

See Conybeare and Howson : *Life and Writings of Saint Paul,* vol. i. page 303.

NOTE 4, page 156.

. . . " those Strangers four."

The three companions of *Saint Paul,* in bearing the Gospel into Europe, were *Silas,* the sharer of his stripes and imprisonment, and the companion of the prison song; *Timothy,* his " own son in the faith," his "dearly beloved;" and *Luke,* " the beloved physician," the beautiful historian of the inspired narrative.

NOTE 5, page 158.

" Come over!—help us!—come!"

"And a vision appeared to Paul in the night; There stood a man of Macedonia, and prayed him, saying, Come over into Macedonia, and help us.

" And after he had seen the vision, immediately we endeavoured to go into Macedonia, assuredly gathering that the Lord had called us for to preach the Gospel unto them.

" Therefore loosing from Troas, we came with a straight course to Samothracia; and the next day to Neapolis;

"And from thence to Philippi . . ."— *Acts,* xvi. 9–12.

A SABBATH MORN AT PHILIPPI.

A.D. 53.

" Therefore loosing from Troas, we came with a straight
course to Samothracia, and the next day to Neapolis ;

" And from thence to Philippi, which is the chief city of
that part of Macedonia, and a colony : and we were in that
city abiding certain days.

" And on the sabbath we went out of the city by a river
side, where prayer was wont to be made ; and we sat down,
and spake unto the women which resorted thither.

" And a certain woman named Lydia, a seller of purple, of
the city of Thyatira, which worshipped God, heard us :
whose heart the Lord opened, that she attended unto the
things which were spoken of Paul."— *Acts*, xvi. 11-14.

A FROWN on old Olympus !

A smile on sunny vale !

A thousand thousand dewdrop globes

Upon the lily's bridal robes,

And on the cistus pale !

Forth from the glowing Eastern
A flood of glory rolled ;
Across the valley's flowery breast,
Across the Thracian mountains' crest,
Right forward to the throbbing West,
In waves like molten gold.

The snow-white mists of morning
Curled heavenward as they spread ;
As if all earth, and sea, and sky
Put on their sabbath drapery ;
All,— save one cloud, opaque and high,
Round old Olympus' head.

Why bend the reeds, low trembling,
Beside the river's lip ?
Is it the footsteps, to and fro,
Of maidens, as they come and go,
With water-urns, down stooping low,
The limpid wave to dip ?

Nay!—for the water lotos

Is anchored still at rest,

And not a ripple filleth up

Her steady alabaster cup,

    Borne on the river's breast.

Yet woman's step hath hastened

Along the reedy side,

And here, this very morn, a draught,

Drawn from the fount of life, is quaffed

    And thirst is satisfied.

Listen! The air is throbbing

As with a life new-born:

And Europe's echoes, to proclaim

The sweetness of a Saviour's name,

    Have wakened up this morn.

There came a stranger herald
From o'er the purple sea,
And on his eager lips he bore
Tidings for Europe's farthest shore,
Life from the dead for evermore—
Light, gladness, victory!

Behold yon group reclining
Amidst the bending reeds!
Think ye that woman's brow ere caught
Such broad expanse of holy thought
From Hellas' fable-creeds?

Think ye that any tidings,
Save those of deathless grace,
Could ever light her heavenward eye
With such a sudden radiancy?—
As if some angel, passing by,
Had smiled upon her face;

And she had smiled in answer,

With glad, yet calm surprise,

The while a casket, locked and sealed,

Had straightway opened, and revealed

A wondrous pearl of price.

Daughter of Thyatira!

Thy soul hath found her quest!

The pearl thou ne'er couldst find enrolled

Amongst earth's purple and her gold,

This very morn — unbought, unsold —

Is clasped upon thy breast!

Christ's chariot-wheels of conquest

Roll not with pomp and din:

The Spirit breathes — and straightway part

The yielding portals of her heart,

And Jesus enters in.

His name, like fragrant incense,

With prayer and praise is blent :—

The great Apostle's living word

This morn the pulse of life hath stirred,

Of a new continent! *

---

* Saint Paul's preaching at Philippi is the first historical record of the proclamation of the Gospel in Europe.

JEPHTHAH'S DAUGHTER,

JUDGES, CHAP. XI.

" The daughter of the warrior Gileadite ;
  A maiden pure, as when she went along
From Mizpeh's towered gate, with welcome light,
  With tabret and with song."—TENNYSON.

By cedar mount and by cypress glen

Hath passed the tramp as of armèd men ;

And Minnith's ripened sheaves were crushed,

And the vintage-bowers of Heshbon flushed

    Deep red—but not with wine !

And the priests of Chemosh looked aghast,

And the idols quaked as the troop swept past,

And the battled gates of Aroer reeled ;

And, on splintered lance and dinted shield,

    The tears of morning shine.

And the Gileadite, with a weary hand,

Hath wiped the gore from his reeking brand ;

And with fierce, glad eye, and haughty brow,

He hath looked tow'rds heaven and read a vow

    He vowed before the fight.

With haughty brow and defiant eye

He reads that vow in the arching sky.

Warrior ! why start at the crimson glow ?

It was but the morning's ruddy flow

    Which poured that blood-red light !

O'er Arnon's stream, and by Jabbok's ford,

Ebbed the host of Jephthah and the Lord :

From silent shrine, and from wailing town,

Where the pride of Ammon lies smitten down,

    Like a reed before the gale.

By cedar mount and by cypress glen,

Rolled back the tramp as of armèd men,

Till the balmy gales of Gilead swell

The floating banners of Israel,

      Amid her olives pale.

Amid her olives pale — near Mizpeh's tower —

Hiding her sweetness — droops a lily flower,

Waiting the warrior's coming smile ; — as pause

Spring-buds for summer, ere they ope their vase

And pour forth perfume. — Jephthah's only child

Had grown amongst the lilies of the wild,

By the same sunlight nectar-stored as they,

By the same dewdrops nurtured day by day,

By the same balmy breezes softly fanned,

Till seemed she sister of the lily band.

Sister — yet queen ! — so stately towered her stem !

So royally hath beauty's diadem

Touched her young brow ! — too soft, too childlike yet

To bear the crown with all its diamonds set !

The wildwood knew her footstep.   The gazelle

Would stand and watch her at the palmy well,

Dipping her pitcher — with his soft, wild eye

Resting on hers.   The bulbul would reply

To the rich, flute-like warble of her note,

With his best trill, before his voice could float

Over the maiden's.   From the fragrant myrtle,

When her light step danced past, the brooding turtle,

Bridling its neck, would coo, in gentle swells,

A welcome to the dancer's timbrel bells.

And when, at eve, oft bent her listening ear

To catch her sire's proud footfall drawing nea

Leaning to meet him from the rude verandah,

Amidst the trellis of the oleander,

The fire-flies glanced, as if in fond caresses,

O'er the soft braidings of her ebon tresses.

Thus grew she.   And her sire — that haughty man,

Whose brow had burned beneath the exile's ban,

Well nigh forgot, charmed by her soft control,

That the hot iron e'er had scorched his soul.

Like a tall cedar by the lightning scarred,

With a stern fate his strong will grappled hard,

And waved defiance to the tempest's wing,

And budded fresh at breathing of the spring,

And spread his boughs to catch the dewdrops sweet,

To filter o'er the lily at his feet !

But mute the timbrel bells, and hushed the dance,

And troubled grew her forehead's smooth expanse,

(Like rippling lake, just ere the threads of mist

Have wove the storm-cloud, and the breeze hath kissed

Its surface, leaving still its depths unstirred)

When stooped she, like a willowy reed, to gird

Her father's sword upon his thigh, and shook

The dust from off his plume.   One long, long look —

And he was gone !   The lily closed her urn

With the sun's setting — till his beams return.

" When will he come ?   I've searched the glowing east,

With gaze as earnest as the sun-god's priest

Watching for morning.   With an aching eye,

I've swept the fiery arch of southern sky,

Yet hailed no glint of lance, no corselet's glare,

No snow-white pennon floating in the air.

I've hearkened for the victor-song, until

My fancy heard it in the gushing rill,

And voice of bird, and harping touch of breeze

Sweeping the branches of the mulberry trees !

When will the conqueror come ?   No mighty foe,

Oh, warrior Gileadite ! could lay *thee* low ;

No Gentile arm could draw the fatal sword

Against the strength of Jephthah—and the Lord !

" But, hark !   'Twas *not* the voice of gushing stream,

Nor bird, nor breeze !   'Twas *not* the noontide's gleam

On silvery birch-stems !—nay ! I know that song !

I know those pennons as they stream along !

I know that plume which waves above the lines,

Like a tall cedar midst a grove of pines!

I know that choral air!   No gentile tongue

Hath e'er profaned its holiness, or flung

Its glory o'er *their* banners.   Egypt's sea

Once moaned its echo.   Listen! ' *Gloriously*

The Lord hath triumphed!'   Hush!— It dies away!

Breathe low, O summer wind!   Thy treble stay,

O shrill-voiced bird!   Again the swelling strain

Reaches its higher notes,—' *The Lord shall reign*

For ever and for ever! '

        " Maidens sweet!

Come forth, with timbrel and with dance, to meet

The mighty man of valour!   Nay, sweet singers!

Draw back one moment!   Let his daughter's fingers

Sound his first welcome!   Let *my* step alone

Dance forth to meet him, o'er his threshold stone!

Forgive my boldness!— he hath only me!

' *Sing to the Lord, who triumphed gloriously!*
The horse and rider He hath thrown — hath thrown ! '

" My father! Oh, my father !"

But a groan

Brake from that strong man's breast — as if Despair

Kept his fell court, and shook his sceptre there !

And the broad cedar quivered 'neath her clasp,

Like a reed shaken in the tempest's grasp.

" My father ! Oh, my father ! My embrace

Hath troubled thee ! Perchance thy daughter's face

Hath lost its roselight — through the long, long yearning,

And lonely vigil, for my sire's returning ?

Ah, thou wilt hail the roselight flowing back,

In a swift current o'er thy homeward track !

What mean these words so hollow, faint, and slow —

' *Alas, my daughter ! thou hast brought me low ?* '

Thy lips *once* breathed, but *only once*, till now,

Such greeting. . Fifteen springs agone, when thou

Wept o'er a new-born babe (a wailing thing !)

Who crossed, upon life's threshold, the white wing

Of 'parting mother—*then* thou whisperedst slow

' Alas, my daughter ! thou hast brought me low !'

(So said they.)   'Twas but once.   And since that hour

Thou hast poured forth upon thy child such dower

Of love so rich, I deemed the golden ore

Would last my lavish need for evermore ! "

The maiden paused.   Then, suddenly, her plaint

(The sobbing voice, subdued, and low, and faint,)

So changed ; that they who wept the while they listened,

Stood breathless.   And a strange, wild glory glistened

On her expanded brow,—*now* firm to bear

The beauty-crown, with every diamond there !

No longer, now, a frail and trembling vine,

Throwing her tendrils round the Strong to twine,

At her full height she rose, sublime and calm.

Erect, majestic, as the stately palm.

" Father!   Shall Jephtha's daughter dare withhold,

From the Lord's work, the silver and the gold,

The onyx and the jacinth ?   Without falter

Thy lamb shall come, unsmitten, to the altar ;

And yield, unbound, untethered, her young life,

Bending her neck to meet the slayer's knife.

If thou have oped thy mouth unto the Lord,

Do with thy child according to thy word !

One boon I crave.   The firstling lamb is parted.

A little season from the joyful-hearted,

Ere it be subject to the priestly eyes,

And sealed, as spotless, for the sacrifice.

Part me from *thee*, my Father ! from all bands

That draw me *down*,— not *upward!*—all that stands

Eclipsing Heaven from earth !   And ere I die,

Let me bewail my young life's elegy

On the lone mountains ; till, amidst that wail,

Heaven's sponsal hymn of love my virgin heart may hail!

*   *   *   *   *   *

*   *   *   *   *

The oleander wildly grew, untrimmed,

Around a voiceless home.   The bulbul hymned

His song, without a rival.   The gazelle

Waited and wondered, at the palmy well.

The turtle stretched her neck, but breathed no answer

To tuneful timbrel, or to timbrel dancer.

The storm-clouds, on the bleak and lonely mountains,

Drew back their shadows.   And the torrent fountains

Poured silvery cadences ; as Gilead's daughters

Wove their sweet wailings with the voice of waters.

And ever and anon a choral key

Burst from their Leader so exultingly,

All other voices paused in breathless wonder,

And brake their sad elegiac bands in sunder,

And strained their quavering voices hopelessly,

To reach the glory of their Leader's key.

Heaven's angels marvelled, as they swept their strings,

And domed the mountain with their radiant wings,

Sheltering the maiden's head.   Perchance the haze,—

The dim, wild twilight of her early days,—

Had parted : and she glimpsed the life immortal,

And the Sin Offering, ready at the portal!

ELIEZER AT THE FOUNTAIN.

GENESIS, CHAP. XXIV.

'Twas the golden hour of sunset,
When the palm beside the well
Waveth o'er the fainting lilies ;
And the desert amaryllis
Shutteth up its crimson bell.

'Twas the hour when myrrh and cassia
Drop their fragrant tears of balm ;
And when Padan-aram's daughters
Come to draw the cooling waters,
From the well beneath the palm.

Who art thou, O Syrian stranger !

With that meekly-thoughtful brow ?

Heeding not the cool breeze, stealing

Softly o'er thy camels, kneeling

    'Neath the palm-tree's feathery bough ;

With their thirsty nostrils quivering

To inhale the fountain's breath ;

And the patient eyes, soft glistening ;

And the drooping ears quick-listening

    To the bubbling sound beneath !

Calm, and motionless, and viewless,

Though his lips be seen to move,

Stands that Stranger,—and converses

With a viewless Fount of mercies,—

    With a living Well of love.

Ah ! that lofty heavenward vision,

And that brow, sublimed with thought,

Be not of the earth's poor moulding,

Nor of nature's own unfolding,

But from holier impress caught.

He hath washed the feet of Angels,

While the reverent knee he bent ;

He hath spread the banquet lowly,

For the heavenly and the holy,

By his master's desert tent.

He hath seen a lordly heirship

Court his grasp,—yet pass him by ;

He hath viewed the wild flower blossom

On the bondmaid's swarthy bosom,

Flushed with pride ; nor heaved a sigh.

He hath hailed the Angel-message,

Without mockery or scorn ;

And hath added his poor blessing

To the Princess*-wife's caressing,

   When the seed elect was born.

He hath watched the child of promise

Flourish like the cedar's bough ;

Yea ! and *shuddered*, as he noted

A mysterious cloud that floated

   O'er his master's reverent brow ;

When they left the well of Sheba,

Early at the blink of day,

And turned northward, to Moriah,

With the wood — the knife — the fire —

   But no firstling lamb to slay !

He hath hailed the home returning ;

And hath marked on either face,

* " Sarah," in the Hebrew, signifies " Princess."

A strange joy ; a holy sweetness ;

As of men who *proved* the meetness,

And the glory and completeness

Of the covenant of grace.

Now behold, on trustful mission,

(Vowed in truth,—in faith obeyed,)

Just ere Padan-aram's daughters

Came to draw the limpid waters,

He hath reached the palm-tree's shade.

Wafted like a breath of incense,

Heavenward flew his wingèd thought ;

Yea ! and there was incense blending

With the prayer to heaven ascending,

From a holier censer caught.

Ere the whispered prayer was uttered,

It was registered on high ;

Almost ere the words were spoken,

Almost ere he asked the token,

   Lo! the answer draweth nigh!

Drawing nearer,— brighter,—clearer,

   Bethuel's daughter comes in sight,

With her pitcher on her shoulder ;

Just as sunset rays enfold her

   In a golden web of light.

Not the brightest maids of Hellas,

   By the blue Ægean sea,

Pressing forth the vine's rich juices —

Not the sweetest of the Muses,

   Dipping draughts from Castaly,—

Not the fairest nymph in Tempe,

With her urn and chorded shell,—

Match this maiden, standing queenly,
Yet so meekly and serenely,
   'Neath the palm beside the well;

In that grand and Eve-like beauty,
Ere the tides of nations crossed,
And the dark world's ruth and evil
Crushed the Eden-type primeval,
   And the shattered fragments lost.

"Drink, my lord!"   In limpid sweetness,
Soft, and angel-like, and clear,
Through the golden ether fluttered
Every syllable she uttered,
   Like rich music to his ear.

"Drink, my lord! and for thy camels
Let me draw the while they drink!"

Oh, each accent that was spoken

Only wrought the outward token

   Of prayer answered, link by link !

Soon the maiden of the fountain

Lit the patriarch's tent with joy !

Soon the Padan-aram lily

Drank the waters, pure and stilly,

   Of the sweet well Lahai-roi !

THE BETTER CHOICE.

MOAB OR ISRAEL?—*Ruth* i.

THE glorious summer sun of Palestine
  Was ripening harvests to a paler gold,
And swelling the rich clusters of the vine,
  In Hebron's gardens, in the days of old ;

When on the hills of Moab paused and stood
  Three wayfarers — and each, across her breast.
Folded the dusky robe of widowhood,
  In silence — as with speechless woe opprest.

One looked as though the heavy hand of time
  Had given weight to sorrow ; but the twain
Were beautiful in womanhood's sweet prime :
  Too new to grief the dregs of woe to drain !

The aged mourner, when she raised her eye
From the rough splinters of the craggy fell,
Looked ever *westward*—where in gladness lie
The balmy vales of blessèd Israel.

One youthful mourner, ever and anon,
Turned *eastward*—where the flocks of Moab feed,
And blithe young shepherds, to the torrent's moan,
Gave back the music of the hollow reed.

The *other* neither looked to east nor west —
Nor back on Moab, nor on Hebron's vale :
But folded her young arms across her breast,
And *heavenward* turned her brow, serene and pale.

What saw she in the broad and blue expanse,
That brought the flush back to her tear-stained face ?
Why stands she, rapt as in some holy trance,
Bathing her forehead in the fount of grace ?

Hath Faith unrolled the secret scroll of time,
   And shown the plucking of a wild, green shoot
From Moab's stock—nursed in a heathen clime,
   And grafted into Israel's chosen root ;

Stretching forth branches, wet with heavenly dew,
   From the sweet vales of hallowed Bethlehem ;
'Till, on her topmost bough, all glorious, grew
   The "*Righteous Branch*" from David's royal stem ?

We know not—but she stood like one whose feet
   Are planted on a Rock which ne'er shall move ;
Girding her heart with high resolve, to meet
   The aged mourner's farewell words of love.

" Turn !—Turn again !—each to thy father's house ;
   Each to thy country's bowers of joy and light :
Each to the bridal train, the loving vows,
   The wedded troth of some young Moabite !

" Turn back, my daughters !—Dwell where ye have dwelt ;
    Under the fruitage of the household vine.
The Lord deal kindly with you, as ye dealt
    Kindly with me—and with your dead, and mine !"

They lifted up their voices—and they weep !
    Tears ! ye be precious as the costliest pearls—
Or, as the transient dews of morning, cheap,
    Which the next zephyr into sunshine whirls.

Both daughters wept !— *One* turned !   Oh, human love !
    'Tis a frail tether which thy fibres twine,
Unless the thread they spin be interwove
    With the immortal cord of love divine !

Back to her country, and her childhood's haunts !
    Back to the wayside brooks, the glad abodes !
Back to the battled tower, the song, the dance !
    Back to her people, and her people's gods !

o

There paused *two* wayfarers on Moab's hills—
 List to that voice which cleaves the liquid air,
With low soft pleadings, falling in sweet trills ;
 Strong in resolve, while meek in lowly prayer !

" Entreat me not to leave thee, nor to turn
 From following thee !   Where thou dost go, I go ;
Where thou dost dwell, I dwell : and meekly learn
 No other people but the Lord's to know.

" Where thou dost die, I die : and sleep beneath
 The balmy dews on Israel's hallowed sod.
Naught shall divide us, save the hand of death !—
 Naught part us—*for thy God shall be my God !*"

Two weary travellers, one eve, came down
 From Moab's hills.   They thread the olive dell,
And pass the cornfields, to the little town—
 Stopping to drink at Bethlehem's cooling well.

THE GLEANER.

Ruth, chap. ii.

Oh, the harvest fields of Bethlehem!
How beauteous to behold
The nodding ear, and the rustling stem,
And the wavy sea of gold!

And the sharpened sickle's flashing glint,
And the reapers, strong and blithe,
And the harvest flowers of many a tint,
And the gleaners, young and lithe!

Oh, the owner of that goodly land,
A thankful man was he,
When he stood amidst the reaper band,
And blessed the company:

And when his servant's benison
　　Benignly he receives,
As he looks around, and passes on,
　　Amongst the yellow sheaves ;

Calling to mind the harvest's Lord,
　　And what He spake of yore,
In many a gracious, loving word,
　　For the stranger and the poor.*

But who is she that bendeth low,
　　With cheek so fair and pale,
Folding across her youthful brow
　　The widow's dusky veil ;

Pacing, with earnest step serene,
　　'Till noon, from early morn,
Down stooping patiently to glean
　　The scattered ears of corn ?

* See Leviticus, xix. 6, and Deut. xxiv. 19, &c.

She never turns to join the laugh
    Of the merry Hebrew maid,
Nor stops the cooling urn to quaff,
    Beneath the plantain shade.

The highborn, Israelitish girl,
    With dark and flashing eye,
Her haughty lip with scorn may curl,
    And pass the stranger by.

The stranger's heart is communing
    With One whose ways are just ;
Beneath the shadow of whose wing
    The friendless came to trust ;

Leaving the bower of childhood's mirth,
    Leaving the natal sod,
For one poor, lonely widow's hearth,
    And for that widow's God :

Grasping His mighty arm, unseen,
  In weakness and in blindness,
And willing trustfully to lean
  Upon His loving-kindness.

" My mother ! let me go, I pray,
  And glean thee bread to eat ;
Mayhap thy God will bless my way,
  And guide my doubtful feet."

Forth went she while the dews of morn
  Still lay, in sparkling gems,
Upon the nodding ears of corn,
  And on the rustling stems.

She happed upon a field to light,
  Which bore a kinsman's name ; —
Who led thee there, young Moabite ? —
  The God of Abraham !

'Twas He, who with His touch of grace
   The rich man's soul did move,
To look upon the stranger's face
   With kindness and with love.

Oh, joy! with ephah full of grain,
   When evening shadows fell,
Again to cross the olive plain,
   And drink at Bethlehem's well ;

And teach the widowed heart to bless
   Her God, for all His ways,
And change the robe of heaviness
   For the comely garb of praise !

THE LITTLE CAPTIVE MAID.

2 KINGS, CHAP. V.

THERE dwelt beneath the pleasant shade
    Of fig-tree and of vine,
A little Israelitish maid,
    In holy Palestine.
It was a land of brooks and springs; —
    A land of corn and wine.

And, kinglike, o'er that watered vale,
    Proud Lebanon looked down,
In mantle fringed with lilies pale,
    And dusky cedar crown;
High in the purple dome of heaven
    Veiling his lordly frown.

I ween 'twas in a pleasant spot,
   This little maid did dwell ;
And softly round her father's cot
   The dews of blessing fell ;
I ween that in this home they loved
   The God of Israel.

She never bent the rebel knee
   'Neath Baal's mystic oak,
Nor bowed her head where, gloomily,
   His impious altars smoke.
She rested in Jehovah's smile,
   And wore His easy yoke.

But He, whose thoughts are not as ours,
   Had higher plans of grace,
And far away from Sharon's bowers,
   Appointed her a place,
Wherein her little lamp might shine
   Amidst a heathen race.

'Twas sunset ;—and a flood of gold
   Had bathed the western fell ;
The flocks were gathered to the fold,
   And watered at the well ;
The turtle nestled o'er her brood,
   Far in the myrtle dell.

But hark !—The neigh of prancing steeds
   Bursts on the stilly air,
And, sweeping o'er the dewy meads,
   Is seen the corslet's glare ;
And flash of sword, and glint of spear,
   Are marked defiling there.

O'er fold and field,—on bower and cot,
   War-horse and rider rushed ;
The dewy breath of night grows hot,
   The vintage bowers lie crushed ;
And, with the life-blood of the slain
   The trodden vines are flushed.

'Tis past!—The fierce marauding band
    Have sheathed the gory glaive,
And swiftly to the Syrian's land
    Rolled back the ebbing wave ;
And the little maid of Israel
    Is captive and a slave !

They counted out the pieces bright
    Of silver and of gold ;
They wrangled o'er the wrong and right,
    In voices harsh and bold ;
And the little bondmaid's tears fell fast,
    As every piece was told.

In gilded cage the captive bird
    Forgets its woodland nest,—
The brooklet by the breezes stirred,—
    The mother's downy breast,—
The shady nook where, cool and clear,
    The pearly dewdrops rest.

But ne'er, I ween, this little maid
  Forgat the lowly cot,
Beneath the vine and fig-tree's shade,
  Where God was unforgot ; —
I ween that from His holy law
  Her heart departed not.

And thrice a-day she open threw
  The lattice of her cell,
And turn'd her gentle face unto
  The land of Israel —
The land wherein her God had said
  His holy Name should dwell.

And thrice a-day she bent her knee,
  And ask'd her God to bless
The lowly bondmaid — and to be
  Strength to the fatherless —
A well-spring in a thirsty land,
  A rest in weariness !

She little knew, while, day by day,
　　A lonely path she trod,
Her humble lamp should show the way
　　That led to Israel's God ;
And that the master, from the slave,
　　Should learn this blessed road.

He was a valiant man of might,
　　And round his princely head
Bright laurels, won in many a fight,
　　Their glorious lustre shed ;
And, in a nation's roll of fame,
　　His honour'd name was read.

Yet, Syrian ! what avails for thee
　　The wreath, the monarch's smile,
While the dire plague of leprosy
　　Thy beauty doth defile ;
And the proud mien and stately brow
　　Are all accounted vile ?

There drops no balm in Syria's land,
   To heal thy fell disease—
No true Physician's potent hand,
   To bring thee health and ease!
Where be thy gods—thy mighty ones—
   Thy idol deities?

In vain, through Rimmon's temple, smokes
   The cloudy censer's breath—
In vain her impious priest invokes
   The name of Ashtoreth!
The only answer is a wail
   Of darkness, hell, and death!

" Oh would to God my master knew
   The prophet that doth dwell
Where softly falls the healing dew
   On favour'd Israel!
He serveth One, whose grace alone
   Can make the leper well!"

'Twas but the breathing of a thought —
 The whisper of a sigh —
And yet thy words, young captive, wrought
 God's will, so mightily,
That there was joy on earth below,
 And joy in heaven on high.

They yoke the chariot to the steeds :
 They form in glittering line ;
They pass the brazen gate that leads
 Tow'rds holy Palestine ; —
They cross the oleander plains,
 And climb the hills of pine.

And from the tall, pavilion'd tower
 Gazed forth that little maid —
Watching, through many a weary hour,
 The moving cavalcade —
Now argent in the glistening sun,
 Now darkening in the shade.

Perchance, with many a gushing tear
  Those gentle eyes were drown'd,
While thought she of the land so dear
  For which that train was bound ; —
And she, like some uprooted flower,
  Left in a thirsty ground !

Alas ! how many a weary night,
  On flagging wing, passed by !
How many a sunset bathed in light
  The glorious western sky !
And from the tall, pavilioned tower
  Still gazed that aching eye !

Hark !—'tis the roll of chariot-wheels,
  The voice of charioteer,
The courser's neigh, the shout, the peals
  Of jubilee and cheer !
And Pharpar and Abana curl,
  In joy, their ripples clear.

The brazen gate is open swung,

   With welcome and acclaim ;

The lattice-shades are backward flung

   By many a Syrian dame :

And round the wayworn chariot-wheels

   Men bow, in low salaam !

And in that chariot standeth one

   Upon whose radiant face

New life, new health, new youth have shone ;

   And where beholders trace

A *strange* expression — beautiful

   With more than nature's grace !

A beauty and a light, ne'er caught

   From Rimmon's lying creed ! —

A solemn grandeur, never wrought

   Of any mortal deed ; —

A bloom and goodliness ne'er sprung

   From any earthly seed !

P

Oh ! he hath found the lowly place
　　Where healing waters roll ;
And he hath reached the Fount of grace
　　Which cures the leprous soul ;
And he hath ventured in, and proved
　　That faith can make him whole.

In Jordan dwelt no virtue rare,
　　No healing power divine ;
(The Syrian streams flowed pure and fair
　　As those of Palestine)—
It was the blood of Christ which cleansed,
　　And Jordan was the sign.

The finger of a little child
　　The way to healing showed ;
'Twas a poor bondmaid's light which smiled
　　Upon that heavenward road :
For there are none too weak—too poor—
　　To point the way to God !

And she who pined for Sharon's bowers —

The sweet, uprooted rose —

Soon opened wide faith's budding flowers.

Where light immortal glows ; —

Transplanted to a holier land.

Where milk with honey flows !

MISCELLANEOUS.

RUNNYMEDE.

'Twas not in hostile phalanx,
   To face some foreign foe,
With spear, and sword, and crested helm,
   And battle-axe and bow,
That the barons of old England
   Each reined his panting steed,
And the British lion shook his mane
   On the field of Runnymede!

No strife for empty glory
   Draws here the glittering brand :
No battle this for ownership
   O'er a few roods of land ;

No struggle for inscribing,

   With blood, a hollow name ;

No fight to win a narrow space

   In the musty rolls of fame ;

But a nation's holy compact

   For liberty and right :

The British lion *will* be free,

   And who dare chain his might ?

Free as the foamy surges

   That lash his ancient rocks ;

Free as the chainless winds that root,

   In storms, his rugged oaks ;

Free as the monarch eagle

   That soars o'er northern mountains ;

Free as the thousand sparkling streams

   That leap from granite fountains !

From many a wall-girt city,

   From many a stately hall,

From many a stern baronial tower.

   With crenellated wall ;

From the orchard lands of Devon,

   From the moorlands of the North,

From Severn unto royal Thames,

   The gallant band rode forth.

From where Northumbria's castles

   Frown o'er the surging deep ;

From where, on meres of Westmorland,

   The mountain shadows sleep ; .

From southern wolds and forests,

   Where wild deer loved to dwell,

And waving harvests gild the field

   Where Saxon Harold fell :

Came many a Norman baron,

   Each with his knightly train,

And many a noble Saxon earl.

   And many an ancient thane :

And, in its jewelled scabbard,

    Was hid the polished brand ;

And stainless banners proudly waved

    In many a strong right hand.

Men, whom dark deadly hatreds

    Had riven long asunder,

Who met not, save, as in the sky.

    Meet lurid clouds of thunder,

Here pledged their haughty greetings,

    And side by side upstood;

And grasped each other's steel-gloved hand,

    In common brotherhood.

Brave Saxon and proud Norman

    Here own *one* stubborn creed—

For a craven king, against his will,

    Keeps tryst at Runnymede !

And ere the golden sunlight,

    Which rose this morn, go down,

A shower of false mock pearls shall fall
    From a recreant monarch's crown ;
And the baldric that shall girdle
    His ermined robe of state,
Shall be fastened with a stronger clasp
    Than a people's fear and hate.

They chose for council chamber,
    No dimly lighted room,
With gold-emblazoned throne of state,
    And purple-broidered dome ;
But the sapphire roof of heaven,
    With its sunlight, free and broad ;
And the broidered carpet that they pressed
    Was England's dewy sward !
And the ancient river rippled
    A smile while flowing on ;
And the summer breeze, in the old oak trees,
    Whispered a benison !

Then stood forth bold Fitzwalter,*

  In his steel-wrought coat of mail ;

And proudly, slowly lifted up

  His barrèd aventayle.

And on his polished hauberk

  His sheathèd sword did ring,

The while, with steady pace, he strode

  Right towards the craven king.

Robed in his crimson tunic,

  With costly jewels set,

And girdled with his golden belt,

  Sat John Plantagenet.

The crown of England tottered

  Upon his crispèd curls ;

And his mantle waved in silken folds,

  Clasped with a brooch of pearls.

* William Fitz-Walter, the Leader of the Barons.

Now speed thee, brave Fitz-Walter!

 Thou graspest in thine hand

A nobler weapon than the blade

 Of thy good Damascus brand;

Thy roll of lettered parchment

 May soil, but ne'er decay;

Thy children's children bless thee still

 For what thou held'st that day!

He knelt, in mute obeisance,

 Upon his mailèd knee.—

And a fresh breeze wakened, and unrolled

 The Charter of the Free!

And a golden sunbeam, falling

 On the ebon and the white,

Made luminous the characters,

 As with a sudden light.

Then paled the King with fury,

 And gnashed his teeth with rage,

The while his quivering eye glanced down

    That mighty parchment's page.

And the grey goose-quill did flutter

    Within his trembling hand,

As, like a cruel pard at bay,

    His stubborn foes he scanned.

But he saw that every scabbard

    Contained a trusty sword ;

And he saw a band of sturdy squires,

    Around each feudal lord ;

And a troop of stalwart yeomen,

    To back each valiant knight,

With cross-bow, spear, and battle-axe,

    All ready armed for fight ;—

So he signed the " Magna Charta :"

    And the royal signet set

On the sole good deed that was ever done

    By John Plantagenet !

And the banner of old England

    Waved proudly from that hour :

And baron, earl, and knight, and squire,

   Spurred back to hall and tower;

Where many a highborn lady

   Kept vigil for her lord,

And waited many a fair-haired girl

   To loose her father's sword.

I ween 'twas joy to listen,

   (When, round the winter's fire,

The matron wrought her tapestry,

   And the daughter touched her lyre,)

To the father's stirring story

   Of the noble band that met,

And fought, and won the bloodless fight

   'Twixt crown and coronet.

The strong old tower shall totter,

   The young oaks shall decay,

But, from the field of Runnymede,

   No glory pass away.

Now hail to the mighty Charter,

    The heirloom of the Free !

And hail to the flag of the Island Queen,

    That waves o'er land and sea !

And hail to each British Mother

    Who nurtures boys as bold,

— *Yet gentler* — than the sturdy band,

    In the good, brave days of old !

" As this was the first effort towards a legal government, so is it, beyond comparison, the most important event in our history, except the Revolution : without which its benefits would have been rapidly annihilated. The Constitution of England has, indeed, no single date from which its derivation is to be reckoned. The institutions of positive law, the far more important changes which time has wrought in the order of society, during 600 years subsequent to the great Charter. have undoubtedly lessened its direct application to our present circumstances. But it is still *the keystone of English liberty.* All that has since been obtained is little more than a confirmation or commentary ; and if every subsequent law were to be swept away, there would still remain the bold features that distinguish a free from

a despotic monarchy.   It has lately been the fashion to
depreciate the value of " Magna Charta," as if it had sprung
from the private ambition of a few selfish Barons, and
redressed only some feudal abuses.   .   .   .   An equal dis-
tribution of civil rights to *all classes* of freemen forms the
peculiar beauty of the Charter."— HALLAM, *Middle Ages*,
vol. ii. p. 446.

PHILIPPINA WELSER.

A FEW miles from Innsbruck, on the road to Salzburg, stands the battlemented castle, " Schloss Ambras," the ancient residence of the Archdukes of the Tyrol. Many an old historic memory peoples its dismantled halls; but the one single episode which endears the place is the embalmed memory of the fair Philippina Welser, the wife of Ferdinand, Count of Tyrol, son of the Emperor Ferdinand I. She is still the ideal genius of the place. " Whose was this old virginal, so carefully kept, and duly dusted?" " Philippina Welser's!" " Whose this little, quaint work-box, with its rusty tambour needles and bodkins?" " Philippina Welser's!" " Whose work was that piece of faded embroidery?" " Philippina Welser's!" " Whose was that suit of armour?" " Ferdinand's, the husband of Philippina Welser?" " Whose chamber is this? whose oratory?" " Philippina Welser's!" " But who was Philippina herself?" " She was the most beautiful woman of her time; the sweetest and the best: the daughter of a simple citizen of Augsburgh." " But how did she become an Archduchess? and how came she here?" " There was a Diet of the Empire at Augsburgh, in 1550; and the young Ferdinand, then only nineteen, caught sight of the beautiful girl, and loved her. She was not lightly won. But, at last, they were secretly married, and Ferdinand brought his bride here, to his hereditary castle, where they lived together in rare, connubial happiness, for thirty-one years. The old Kaiser was furious at his son's *mésalliance;* and, for eight years, would listen to no entreaty for reconciliation. But the same beauty, which had once charmed the son to love, at length charmed the father to forgiveness. One day, a beautiful stranger, leading a princely boy in either hand, threw herself at the Emperor's feet, and claimed and gained his parental love.

" PHILIPPINA, rose of Augsburgh!

 Blooming on thy stem, alone!

Wherefore turn thee from the homage

 Of thy noble Kaiser's son?"

" I am but a burgher's daughter,

 And the brow thou callest fair

Never fashioned was, nor moulded

 Ducal crown of pearls to wear.

Never have my maiden musings

 Stolen beyond my father's hall;

Plying swift my tambour needle,

 Playing soft my virginal!

And the wildest of my visions

 Was, beneath the matron coif,

To confine these vagrant tresses

 As a simple burgher's wife!

Thou, whose cradle was empanelled

 With the Double Eagle's wings;

And whose purple line hath mingled

 Ever with the blood of kings;—

All *thy* visions should be lofty;

 Soaring proud,—as eagles sail:—

All *my* thoughts are meek and lowly;

 Like the cushat's of the vale.

Turn thee to the Kaiser-palace:—

 Seek some noble, lily hand:—

Some fair bride, whose high aspirings

 Throb with thine, brave Ferdinand!

Nay! I know what thou would'st answer:

 Yet this face thou callest bright,

And these locks thou stylest golden,

 Soon must lose their bloom and light.

How will, then, the crown archducal

 Grace a brow of faded bloom?

Tell me : will the 'rose of Augsburgh'

 Never lose her first perfume?

Now, she blushes in youth's morning;

 And the dew is in her cup.—

Listen! Soon the breath of noontide

 Will have scorched her beauty up.

Then, perchance, the pale rose, withered,

 Will be flung away—to die"—

But the noble blood of Hapsburg

 Flushed his cheek and fired his eye,

And he rose, erect, before her;

 And he leaned upon his brand :—

" By this good sword of my fathers,

 And the word of Ferdinand,

Not thy grace, nor bloom, nor beauty,
   —Angel-passing though they be,—
Could have won my loyal homage,
   Or have bent this mailèd knee!
These are but the crystal casket,
   And the jewel, shining through,
Will outlast the shivered crystal,
   Beautiful, immortal, true!
Let the diamond, first and purest,
   In my father's ' kaiser-kron,'
Weighed against this matchless jewel,
   Lightly, to the winds be thrown!
Philippina! Sweetest! Dearest!
   Wear, for *me*, the matron coif:
And forget the wreath archducal
   In the bosom-friend and wife."

So she oped the jewel-casket,
   And she tendered him her love.

And the bridal flowers were gathered,

   And the bridal veil was wove.

And he led her to his castle,

   In the valley of the Inn ;

Where a guard of giant mountains

   Girdled her from strife and din.

And her goodness and her beauty

   Lighted up the gloomy pile,

To the gladness of a palace;—

   To the glow of summer's smile !

Dark the angry flush that passes,

   Slowly, o'er the Kaiser's face :

" Never will I own as daughter

   Maiden of the burgher race !

Never yet hath shield been quartered,

   With the proudly plumèd wings

Of the empire's Double Eagle

   But from ancient line of kings !"

So she meekly bowed to duty,

   Gladdened by her consort's love ;

While she charmeth grief to gladness

   Wheresoe'er her footsteps move.

Lightening every peasant's burden

   With her bounty and her grace :

Bending o'er her babies' cradle,

   Angel-like, her radiant face.

    *   *   *   *   *

      *   *   *   *

Who is this, O haughty Kaiser !

   Matron-like, yet passing fair,

Blushing, like the almond's blossom,

   Midst a cloud of golden hair ?

With a boy of princely bearing,

   Left and right, on either side,

Like the royal house of Hapsburg,

   (Curling lip, and eagle-eyed !)

Kneeling low, and kneeling lowly ;

   Pleading soft, in broken tone,

" Kaiser ! let me call thee *'Father !'*
　Bless the children of thy Son !"

Like the passing of a shadow
　From some Alpine peak of snow,
At the rosy kiss of sunshine,
　O'er his brow there came a glow,
Warm, as in our life's young morning ;
　And he pressed her to his heart ;
Whisp'ring,—" Deign to be my daughter ;
　Angel-spirit though thou art !"

Did she linger in the palace,
　Blazing like a star of light,
With the pearly crown archducal
　Sparkling on her forehead bright ?
Nay ! the fortress of her early
　Wedded life of quiet love,
(Where the bridal veil was folded,
　And the matron coif was wove ;

Where the cradle of her babies
    Glowed with many an Eden-thought,—
Bud, and fruit, and bird, and blossom,
    By her tambour needle wrought,)
There the home is, where her spirit
    Nestled lowly,—love-secure ;
Midst the honour of the humble
    And the homage of the poor ;
'Till the angels came to take her,
    Long before the shades of even,
To the pearl gates of a city,
    Where her heart found rest—and Heaven !

A GOOD-FRIDAY LEGEND.

A.D. 33.

" Old things are passed away."

Plutarch mentions a tradition, according to which, at the hour of the Saviour's agony, a wailing cry, like the dying of the false gods, swept across land and sea, in the hearing of certain mariners : *and so the oracles ceased.*

A MAIDEN of the classic South,

   In regions fancy-haunted,

Sang a wild story—half in truth,

But half the mythic dream of youth ;—

   And thus her tale she chaunted.

" The helm was shipped,—the sail unbraced,
    At daylight's rosy dawning ;
And o'er the rippling waves he chased
    The footsteps of the morning.

" I heard the lapping of the tide,
    Down in the glen of myrtles,
Where he had lingered at my side
    To listen to the turtles.

" With oar, and sail, and fisher's net,
    His buoyant barque was freighted :—
'Twould bear him back ere Phœbus set,
    Unless he were belated.

" I heard the Nereid's merry shout,
    Within their oozy hollow ;
I saw them dip and plunge about
    His nimble boat to follow.

" The sea-green Oceanides

    Were joining in their laughter ;

And, floating o'er the crimsoned seas,

    Were trooping blithely after.

" I danced upon the pebbly beach ;

    I sang with wildered pleasure ;

For well I knew they could not reach

    My own betrothèd treasure.

' I turned me to the ilex grove ;

    Where dews were round me weeping ;

And in a bower the shadows wove

    I caught the Dryads sleeping.

" They slept like tranced, insensate things,

    That ne'er expect a waking ;

And then I heard the rush of wings,

    And felt a sudden shaking !

" I heard, beneath the white cascade,
 The reed-crowned Naiads splashing ;
And started, in the laurel shade,
 At silvery pinions clashing.

" I marked a pale light through the gloom,
 But saw no clearer vision :—
It might have been mild Hermes' plume,
 On some Olympian mission.

" But just as evening's saffron train
 With night's dun vesture mingles,
I heard my fisher's barque again
 Upon the pebbly shingles.

" I sang my greeting clear and strong,
 But caught no tuneful answer ;
I chaunted loud my sweetest song,
 But heard no choral stanza.

" Perchance it was the evening's chill
  Which dimmed that radiant forehead ;
And sealed that lip, so pale and still,
  And blanched the cheek so florid.

" He brought no gift of ruby stem
  From ocean gardens floral ;
Nor pearly shell, nor sparkling gem,
  Nor rosy frond of coral.

" We sat beneath an ancient pine,
  So weird, and scathed, and hoary ;
And while I grasped his hand in mine,
  He told his wondrous story."

THE MARINER'S STORY.

" ' The helm was shipped,—the sail unbraced,
  At daylight's rosy dawning;

And o'er the rippling waves I chased
  The foosteps of the morning.

" ' But soon there slowly, slowly fell,
  A hush o'er sky and ocean ;
As if all nature owned one spell
  Of breathless, strange emotion.

" ' The veilèd chariot of the sun
  Was darkened in high heaven,
Though scarcely yet three hours were run
  From noontide on to even.

" ' The spirits of the air and sea
  All seemed to pause and languish ;
Held in mysterious sympathy
  With some immortal anguish.

" ' As though they watched, with love intense,
  Gasping, and wan, and breathless,

A fainting of Omnipotence —

    A dying of the deathless!

" ' The shores grew dim ;— the sweltering sky

    And moaning ocean darkened :

And then a voice came floating by,

    And I bowed down—and hearkened.

" ' It floated through unmeasured space,

    By distance undiminished ;

So awful—yet so full of grace

    It sounded —" IT IS FINISHED !"

" ' I heard Olympian palace-halls

    Slam home their ivory portals :

I heard the thyrsis as it falls

    From gasping, weird immortals.

" ' *Immortals?* Nay! a *mortal* cry

    Arose amid the silence ;

Answered by wails of agony,
   From sea, and shore, and islands.

      .

" ' From glen to cliff,—from bay to creek,
   A sobbing and a sighing ;
From vale to mount, a wildered shriek
   As of the frore and dying !.

" '*Finished!*   Jove's palace-gates no more
   Will ope to hail the morrow :
I knew the age of dreams was o'er,
And the sweet Muses wept full sore,
   Yet felt I ruth nor sorrow.

" ' Perchance there dawns a golden age,
   More bright than gilded trances ;
When Truth shall ope a holier page
   Than poets' sweetest fancies.

" ' Though bright Apollo ne'er again
    Shall mount his chariot golden,
His steeds will tramp that azure plain
    By mightier force upholden.

" ' Though queenly Dian drop her bow
    Upon the dreamy mountain,
The moonlight still shall overflow
    Its silver-brimmèd fountain.

" ' And spring's young flowers will bud and blush
    Without the breath of Flora ;
And morning's rosy light outflush
    The fingers of Aurora.

" ' The playful Nereids' winding shells
    Are hushed in hollow silence ;
But Ocean's organ-voice still swells
    Around his caverned islands.

" ' And not a reed or flower will mourn

One pleasant brook's cessation,

Though the sweet Naiad's broken urn

Hath poured its last libation.

" ' And spirits blend in harmony,

And love is strong for ever,

Though Cupid be a phantasy,

And emptied be his quiver.

" ' Perchance there is a mightier Hand

Than Jove's — to hold the thunder ;

Perchance a kingly Throne shall stand,

Though his be rent in sunder.

' 'Ancient of Days,—whose dateless morn

Is timeless and eternal ;

Elder than Chronos ! — an Unborn,

Whose Godhead is supernal.

" ' *Finished!*   The word was mystery ;

 And clouds are intervening ;

But faith is waiting for the key

 To comprehend its meaning.' "

AN OLD VERGER'S TALE.

When Queen Victoria visited Potsdam, in 1858, it happened that the old Verger, who showed her the tomb of Frederick the Great, was the same man who had showed the same shrine to Napoleon Buonaparte in 1805. When the Soldier-Emperor visited the Soldier's grave, the sword of the Dead was still kept as a national relic on the iron tomb. It was seized by the hand of Napoleon, and sent as a trophy of conquest to Paris; nor has it ever been restored to Prussia.

He placed his foot on that marble stone;

　The man whose name had passed

Over Europe, like the thunder's moan,

　And like the lightning's blast.

I heard the ring of his spur of steel,

　As, with quick and stubborn tread,

And folded arms, he set his heel

　By the tomb of our royal Dead.

The lamplight fell, as it falleth now,

    Through the chill of an autumn morn,

On his marble cheek and moveless brow,

    And chiselled lip of scorn.

I thought me, with a speechless dread,

    That the flags beneath me stirred ;

But the tomb lay moveless o'er our Dead,

    And on the tomb — the sword !

We sighed no word, we raised no hand,

    When the Stranger's arm of fate

Stretched forth — and grasped the hilted brand

    Of the man we called " *The Great !* "

For the Prussian Eagle, in her woe,

    Forgat, one hour, her truth ;

And her swarthy wing was drooping low,

    And her eye was dulled with ruth.

And the foeman triumphed ! — for he saw

    The strong forget her might ;

Loosening the orb from her left claw,

    And the sceptre from her right ;

And a hundred thousand victors dashed
   Through our opened gates that day ;
And a hundred thousand lances flashed,
   In long and bright array.
And banners streamed, and clarions blew,
   And the Gallic Eagle's wings
Were fluttering o'er a retinue
   Of false or subject kings.

Not long !—for the free Black Eagle rose
   In the strength of her ancient trust ;
And she rent the banner of her foes,
   And dragged it through the dust.
And she burst the Frank's imperious chain,
   And his Eagles sped their flight ;
For orb and sceptre were firm again
   In left claw and in right.

Aye !   Fifty summers have come and flown,
   And we garnered in their sheaves ;

And fifty autumns breathed their moan
 Among the withered leaves ;
And fifty times have the Christmas chimes
 Rung in new hope and trust,
Since that stubborn heel, with its spur of steel,
 Stood by our royal dust.

They said it once was joy to scan
 My boyhood's ringlets bright :—
You smile as you gaze on the bent old man,
 With his locks of snowy white.
Morn's orient tide,—noon's surging wave,
 Have flowed across my head ;
Yet still I watch by the soldier's grave,
 And pray by the kingly dead.
I have seen the glowing sunrise steep
 The floor with its crimson stain ;
I have watched the golden evening creep
 Adown that amber pane ;

I have marked the scutcheons' blazoned hues
   Grow pale and grey with time ;
And I've seen the chiselled marbles lose
   The whiteness of their prime :
But I still kept vigil, as of yore,
   Amid the vaulted gloom,
When a Royal Stranger stood, once more,
   Beside our royal tomb.

She stood upon that self-same stone ; —
   The Queen whose name hath passed
Around the world, like the dulcet tone
   Of a silver clarion's blast.
She stood,—with a hushed, yet queenly tread ;
   In silence,—as in prayer :
With a drooping eye and a bending head,
   With its softly braided hair ;
With lips which little babes have kissed,
   As cheek to cheek they lean ;

And a brow where princely sons ne'er missed

    The *Mother*—in the *Queen*.

She wore no jewelled diadem,

    No ermine robe trailed she ;

A woman's tear was her single gem,

    And her robe was charity.

No coat of mail, with its galling fold,

    Across her free heart pressed :

Her people's love is the shield of gold

    Which guards that queenly breast.

Oh happy isle where the roses smile

    Around her palace tower,

Where bloomed a rare sweet Bud to spare

    For the royal Prussian's bower !

We ask no sword on the Soldier's tomb,

    To keep our country free ;—

The English Rose, with her true perfume,

    Our sweet defence shall be !

CHIMINGS.

The Beautiful and Dutiful!
  Oh rend them not in twain;
They be but sister links that hang
  Upon a golden chain.
The hand that rends the Beautiful
  From off its sister ring,
Will find, within its reckless grasp,
  A hollow, worthless thing.

The Beautiful and Dutiful,
  By balmy breezes fanned,
Through light and shade, unconsciously,
  Move heavenward, hand in hand:
They smile into each other's eyes,
  The while they pace along,

And exiles both from Paradise,

    They sing the Eden song.

The Beautiful and Dutiful!

    Oh, it is sweet to trace

Their work, in lovely unison,

    On gesture, form, and face.

The brow which grace is moulding fair,

    In Duty's gentle school,

Though bloom nor symmetry be there,

    Is passing beautiful !

The Youthful and the Truthful!

    Their bands should ne'er be riven ;

For they were one in Edenland,

    And they are one in Heaven.

And every heart where Jesus dwells,

    — Himself the glorious " Truth,"—

Is watered by ten thousand wells

    Of fresh and fadeless Youth.

The Holy and the Lowly!

No hand may dare to sever
The bond that binds them into one,
For ever and for ever!
According to the heavenward pace
At which the saint grows holy,
So, by the lamblike Saviour's grace,
He groweth meek and lowly.

The Holy and the Lowly!

They be not twain — but one;
Eternal their identity,
And cannot be undone.
They be like Jacob's shining road,
Wherein our faith can scan
Thy work, O holy Son of God,
And lowly Son of man!

TO CECILIA.

'Tis said, in legendary lore,
By Tyber's bank dwelt one of yore
Who the sweet name thou bearest, bore.

Cecilia!   And her brow was bright,
All radiant with celestial light,
Untouched by care, or stain, or blight!

And wheresoe'er she moved along,
The Angels, in a viewless throng,
Stooped down,—and listened to her song.

And as they shook the martyr's palm
Across her brow, sweet drops of balm
Fell there, and spread a holy calm.

And, now and then, an Angel's wing
Would sweep across some flagging string,
And wake a more ecstatic ring.

Whate'er the cadence of the tone,
They say the key-note was but one,
And this it was,—" *Thy will be done!*"

And thou, her namesake! on whose bloom
The shadowy palm of martyrdom
Will never cast its solemn gloom ;

Thy lot it is to seek and find
The Beautiful with Truth combined ;
And, serving God, to serve thy kind.

Life's common lessons can inspire
Tunes sweeter than the sweetest wire
That throbbed in Saint Cecilia's lyre.

When duties move in sweet accord,

And actions harmonise with word,

And thoughts lie subject to the Lord.

Thus, in thy daily life's routine,

Though clouds opaque may intervene,

Bright Angels watch thee, though unseen.

And when thou haltest in thy song,

And jarring notes rise high and strong,

In discord betwixt right and wrong ;

Perchance the wafting of their wing

A cooling breath of life may bring

Across the jarred or broken string ;

And tune it into song again,

Until thy spirit catch the strain,

And carry out the sweet refrain.

S

But soon the day shall dawn, when thou

Amidst the Angel-choir shalt bow,

With the saint's halo round thy brow ;

Singing the anthem thou hast known

On earth, but in its feeblest tone,—

" *For ever, Lord, Thy will be done!*"

THE BABE AND THE SAINT.

We do not say, " Alas, how soon !" when, in morn's
  golden hour,
The folded, dewy bud bursts forth a bright and
  glorious flower ;
We do not question, " Wherefore thus?" when borne
  on radiant wing,
The Psyche rises from its thrall, a living, glorious
  thing :
And yet how many a heavy sigh from aching bosoms
  broke,
When the Babe Katie fell asleep—and the Saint
  Katie woke !

Oh! Baby Katie was a sweet and winsome thing
    for earth !

A hundred happy smiles broke forth at tidings of
    her birth ;

And trebled generations grouped to fondle earth's
    new guest ;

And gentle arms have caught new skill in cradling
    her to rest :

And prayers have blent, at morn and eve, with glad
    thanksgiving strain,

Because the sweet Babe Katie comes to join the
    pilgrim train.

On right hand and on left, life's thorns were softly
    swept aside,

And Katie's teardrops, ere they fell, with kisses warm
    were dried ;

And every grief was charmed away before it left its
    trace

Upon the placid sweetness of the dimpled baby face ;

And flowers were wreathed, in festal guise, where'er
    she passed along ;
And every smile was met with smiles, and every song
    with song !

It would not do !   Those tender feet were never
    called to move,
Save o'er the jasper floor within the courts of
    heavenly love.
That small, soft hand was never framed to grasp the
    pilgrim staff ;
That rosy lip was never meant from wayside brook to
    quaff ;
Nor that sweet silvery voice to blend with any mortal
    hymn ;—
Its tones be destined for the choir of waiting
    Seraphim !

What marvel, then, if Katie rose at golden peep of day,
Just tasted of the wayside brook, then sighed, and
    turned away ?

What marvel if there shone a light within her earnest
    eye,

As if she saw the radiant wings of angels drawing
    nigh?

What wonder if there swept a shade across her infant
    brow,

As from the viewless wafting of a palm's victorious
    bough?

So the Babe Katie fell on sleep! The silver cord
    was riven!

But the Saint Katie wakened up! and there was joy
    in heaven!

And at the glorious melody of one victorious Name,

The gates of pearl, to let her in, flew back with glad
    acclaim;

And she hath learned to speak *that Name*,—to praise
    that untold grace,

Before her unknown Saviour's throne,—before her
    Father's face.

And doth she sometimes bend her down to scan that
    spot on earth,

Made beautiful for evermore by sweet Babe Katie's
    birth?

And doth she sometimes stoop, and breathe a voice-
    less whispering;

And fan her mother's pale sweet brow with soft and
    viewless wing;

And charm away that exile look of sorrow and of
    care;

And smile a golden beauty o'er that little lock of hair?

We know not! But we know that He, from whom
    the Child-gift came,

Who writ, within the book of life, the Saint's new
    heavenly name,

Will fill with gladness and with song the void and
    silent place,

And lighten up the darkness with the shining of His
    face;

'Till Sire and Mother bless their God, beneath the
    chastening stroke,
For the Babe Katie, fallen asleep — and for the
    Saint who woke!

A SABBATH REMINISCENCE.

WE stood together, side by side,
  Sweet Eleanor and I.
Alas! a holier Sabbathtide,
  To her was drawing nigh.

With dulcet voice, subdued and calm,
  She read, in solemn tone,
The verses of the morning psalm,
  Alternate,— one by one.*

Her golden head was bent beneath
  The holy hush of prayer ;
" Cast me not off!"   The whispered breath
  Still seemed to linger there ;

* We were reading the 71st Psalm.

As if " old age" had nought to do
    With such a bud as this,
Whereon reposed life's morning hue
    Of softest, purest bliss.

The tender glow of mantling health
    Lay on her cheek of rose ;
And in her eye love's hallowed wealth
    Was shrined, in meek repose.

I listened.   O'er the psalmist's shell
    Lingered the same low tone ;
" Forsake me not when strength shall fail !"
    Murmured that little one.

I marked her form of freest mould ;
    The limbs so round and fair ;
The shining locks, like thredded gold,
    Untouched by time or care.

What hath such prayer to do with *thee?*
    Young dream of joy and love!
Dear lute of sweetest melody,
    Tuned — but for courts above!

God heard her plea.   The blight of age
    Ne'er breathed upon her bloom;
He willed not that earth's pilgrimage
    Should rifle heaven's perfume.

" Forsake me not!"   The whispered prayer
    Soon reached the Father's throne;
Unstained by grief, undimmed by care,
    Jesus resumed *His own.*

———————

She was but nine when she passed into the light of immortality, almost in the twinkling of an eye.

OUR DEPARTED TWAIN.

They were not mine, and yet my heart
    Caressed them as its own,
They seemed to bear so full a part
    In every sight and tone !
Their gladness seemed to blend its light,
    With every beam that shone.

I scarcely know what spell first bound
    My flowing tide of love,
To stay its sweep ; and deepen round
    The bower thy childhood wove,—
Dear, rosy gift of summer joy !
    Dear, softly-pinioned dove !

A fountain was she in life's way,

    Clear, beautiful, and calm ;

And angels round it loved to stay,

    And sing their Eden psalm.

And flowers of sweetness round it bloomed ;

    And odorous plants of balm.

The gentlest breath,—the lightest sigh

    Would stir its depths so clear ;

Each tone of love that whispered by

    An answering voice might hear.

The softest light might find a smile,—

    The faintest sigh a tear.

The meanest flower, the lowliest thing,

    Obtained her ready love.

The household robin, with his wing,

    Would her soft tresses move.

In drawing near to her, he seemed

    No nat'ral fears to prove.

She loved each lowly place serene
　　Where humblest blossoms grew ;
Each little spot of pleasant green
　　Her sweet affections drew.
She loved God's earth—and loved the light,
　　High in His heaven of blue.

The misty hills won not her heart,
　　In distant, towering pride,
Until she viewed them as a part
　　(All fair and sanctified)
Of God's creative love ; *His* work,
　　Who on the cross hath died.

And when she listened to the gush
　　Of their rejoicing springs,
And saw the tender sunshine flush
　　The tempest's lurid wings,
Ah, *then*, the mountains were enrolled
　　Amongst belovèd things.

Yet was she still the playful child,
  With limbs so round and free ;
And step all vigorous and wild ;
  And voice of frolic glee !
And heart brim-full of life's delight,
  And wild-wood ecstasy.

Hush !   'Tis the same dear steps which fall
  With softest, gentlest tread,
Obedient to the faintest call
  Breathed from her mother's bed,
To hand the cup, the pillow smooth,
  Or soothe the aching head.

Hush ! 'Tis the same clear voice, though stilled
  Down to its lowest key,
When wakeful chords of love are thrilled
  By touch of sympathy.
Ah, then, how delicate their tone !
  How soft ! how silvery !

She was not ours.   Lord! she was Thine,
　Who, for a gladdening while,
Didst lend that little lamp, to shine
　Irradiate with Thy smile :
Then placed it in Thy heavenly courts,
　Where nothing shall defile.

Though shadows lie across our way,
　E'er since her light hath fled,
The lamp still burns with holier ray,
　By oil of gladness fed.
She was not ours.   She was His own,
　Who for her ransom bled.

And *thou* wert also His,— not ours,—
　Oh precious Second-born !
Thou sweetest of all fragrant flowers ;
　Thou rose without a thorn !
Thou brightest dewdrop on the spray,
　In spring's most dewy morn !

A sparkling brook ! yet oft unseen,
    As on it blithely welled,
But for a line of living green
    Which marked the course it held ;
And but for tones — sweet tones that rose
    Where'er its ripple swelled.

The thirsting flowers bent down, to kiss
    The fertilizing wave ;
Its chosen course,—its dearest bliss
    To gladden and to lave !
And pleasant, to each passer-by,
    The music which it gave !

Then He, who loved and watched its tide,
    (Himself the Fount of light)
Did send His Spirit down to guide
    Its lovely course aright ;
To deepen its enriching wave,
    And stem it with His might.

T

Alas ! we see that line no more,
Of bright and living green :
Alas ! the buds around its shore,
Of late, athirst have been ;
And the mild blessings of its course
To pilgrim eyes unseen :

For God hath turned our brooklet back
To Zion's fount of love ;
And led it from its earthly track
To urns of light above ;
And Seraphs, in their hymns of praise,
Her choral sweetness prove !

TO MARY.

FIFTEEN springs ago, sweet Mary,
  Came a heavy cloud of woe.
Dark with mystery, and very
  Blighting, seen from earth below :

Very bright and very glorious,
  Seen from Love's own home above ;
Where the angels, in their chorus,
  Paused, as if in raptured love,

To roll back the pearly portal
  Of the heavenly domain,
And receive to bliss immortal —
  Suddenly — thy sisters-twain !

Ah !   Life's roselight and its golden

Paled, and well-nigh vanished *then;*

And the springtide flowers unfolding,

Ne'er have looked the same again.

Yet, amidst the blight and sadness,

Blossomed on the drooping bough,

Soon, a gift of dewy gladness—

And this Maytide gift wert *thou!*

Thus was little Mary reckoned

'Mongst the stricken band on earth ;

Mortals count her but the *second*

Daughter,—*Angels* count her *fourth !*

Both be right !—To thee are given

Duties of a twofold kind ;

And the claims of earth and heaven

Thus be softly intertwined.

Daughter of the loved and living !

    Sister of the saints in rest !

Daughter of the trusting, striving !

    Sister of the crowned and blest !

Daughter ! be thou faithful-hearted

    To the loved, thus sore bereft !

Sister of the bright departed !

    Be thou brightener of the left.

Ever mindful of a *second*

    Daughter's genial place on earth ;

Mindful, too, that thou art beckoned

    Heavenward, as the precious *fourth !*

MY GRANDMOTHER'S WALKING-CANE.

With reverent love I call to mind,
   And picture, o'er again,
The feeble hand which used to rest
   Upon that polished cane.
Things bright and fair dissolve in air,
   And strong wax weak—but ah !
I see *thee*, clear as yesterday,
   My long-lost Grandmamma !

The bonnet, and the silken cloak,
   With quaintly fashioned hood ;
The plaiting of the cambric sleeve,
   Held by its golden stud ;

The ample gown of poplin brown,

   With long and flowing train ;

And the mittened hand which leaned for strength

   Upon the Indian cane.

Alas ! It was a halting step,

   It was a faltering pace ;

But there was love which faltered not

   Upon her gentle face.

And there was light, from out of sight,

   Upon that reverend head,

From regions whither she was bound,

   With firm and steady tread.

I mind me how my young round hand,

   Did love to clear away

The small fir-cones and pebble stones

   That in her pathway lay ;

Scarce wotting half the patient love

   That strove, with soft caress,

To sweep the thorns from off the path
　　Of childhood motherless !

Alas !　The step on gravelled walk
　　Grew rare — and yet more rare ;
And then — instead of staff and shoe,
　　The slow-paced wheeling chair ;
And then — ah me ! they folded up
　　The out-of-doors attire,
And placed the padded elbow chair
　　Beside the chamber fire.

I mind me (how should I forget ?)
　　My footstool at her knee ;
The quiet talk — the dainty cup
　　From which she sipped her tea.
I mind me of the " bon-bon " box,
　　The trinkets, quaint and old ;
And Queen Penelope, embossed
　　On watch of massive gold.

But, more than all, the patient smile —
  The meek and gentle voice —
The whispered "*Hush!*" which quickly checked
  The too hilarious noise —
The listening ear — the ready tear
  For others' grief or pain : —
But wherefore dive for memory's pearls
  Adown life's troubled main ?

There was a sound of startled feet,
  Fast hurrying to and fro,
And then a hush of quietness,
  And movements dull and slow ;
And then — ah, me ! in darkened rooms
  Our tear-drops fell like rain ;
And then they placed aside the chair,
  And put away the cane !

We knew that she was gone to dwell
  Amongst a shining throng,

Where He who was her staff and stay

Is now her strength and song —

Where weakness is exchanged for might,

And shadows fade in truth —

And death in life — and hoary age

In everlasting youth !

HYMN.

" I will bless the Lord at all times."

Oh, Thou, whose bounty fills my cup
  With every blessing meet,
I give Thee thanks for *every drop* —
  The bitter and the sweet !

I praise Thee for the desert road,
  And for the river-side —
For all Thy goodness hath bestowed,
  And all Thy grace denied ! —

I thank Thee both for smile and frown,
  And for the gain and loss ;
I praise Thee for the future crown,
  And for the present cross ! —

I thank Thee for the wing of love
Which stirred my worldly nest,
And for the stormy cloud that drove
The flutterer to Thy breast ! —

I bless Thee for the glad increase,
And for the waning joy ;
And for this strange, this settled peace.
Which nothing can destroy !

THE END.